D0568948

GREAT CHRISTMAS MOVIES

Great Christmas Movies

Frank Thompson

TAYLOR PUBLISHING COMPANY
DALLAS, TEXAS

Copyright © 1998 by Frank Thompson. All rights reserved.

No part of this book may be reproduced in any form or by any means—including photocopying and electronic reproduction—without written permission from the publisher.

Published by Taylor Publishing Company
1550 West Mockingbird Lane
Dallas, Texas 75235
www.taylorpub.com

Library of Congress Cataloging-in-Publication Data
    Thompson, Frank T., 1932–
        American Movie Classics' great Christmas movies / by Frank Thompson
          p. cm.
        Filmography: p.
        Includes index.
        ISBN 0–87833–214–6
        1. Christmas films—United States—History and criticism.
    2. Christmas in motion pictures. I. Title.
    PN1995.9.C5113T56 1998
    791.43'634–dc21

98–39013
CIP

Book design by Mark McGarry
Set in Bodoni

Printed in the United States of America
10   9   8   7   6   5   4   3   2   1

p. ii, Scrooge (Reginald Owen) and Tiny Tim in *A Christmas Carol* (1938).

p. iv, Bing Crosby and Danny Kaye belt out a number in *White Christmas*.

p. xii, Clarence (Henry Travers) tries to convince George Bailey (James Stewart) that he's a guardian angel in *It's a Wonderful Life*.

p. xvi, Edmund Gwenn as Kris Kringle in *Miracle on 34th Street* (1947).

For Alastair Sim
The Once and Future Scrooge

Contents

Acknowledgments

IT WAS CHRISTMAS the year 'round at my house while I was writing this book and writing and directing the special of the same name for American Movie Classics. But I never expected the year to bring me so many brightly wrapped gifts: gifts of friendship, advice, research assistance, and all kinds of help, support and helpful criticism. Here's my list of those who have been particularly nice to me this year; the naughty will remain anonymous.

First, I literally couldn't have completed this book without the help of John Andrew Gallagher. In the final weeks, when I was frantically writing the book and also neck-deep working to complete the AMC special, John stepped forward and offered to write some of the individual film entries for me. Since he is both a wonderful writer and a knowledgeable film historian, I happily took him up on it. John has made a terrific contribution to *AMC's Great Christmas Movies* with his essays on *It's a Wonderful Like*, *Meet Me in St. Louis*, *Three Godfathers*, and a few others, all noted with his initials. John also handled the New York unit for the AMC special and conducted the onscreen interviews with David Huddleston and Darren McGavin. This is my fourteenth book since 1983, and John has been of enormous help and has offered invaluable advice on every single one of them—but never so much as on this one.

Thomas W. Holland has also made incredible contributions to this book. Tom was my producer on the AMC special and has been my partner on many other projects. We so frequently talked over ideas that eventually ended up in both this book and in the special that it's difficult to remember who came up with them first. All I know is, if it weren't for Tom, there would be no special and no book. He's one of the best friends I have and the best collaborator that anyone could ask for.

It was through the good graces—and good taste!—of Nancy McKenna at American Movie Classics that the special was made, and so I owe her a great debt of gratitude. I have worked frequently with Nancy over the past few years and have always found her to be totally professional and totally delightful—a pretty rare combination in this business. I'm proud to know her and to acknowledge my gratitude to and affection for her.

Mike Emmerich, my editor at Taylor Publishing, gave this book the green light, knowing that it would have to be written and produced in an unbearably short time. For giving me the opportunity to write this book, I thank him most humbly. For setting me on a path of total frenzy for months at a time, I'm also grateful–but exhausted.

I also owe a deep, deep debt of gratitude to the staff of the Margaret Herrick Library of the Academy of Motion Picture Arts and Science, particularly Stacey Endres and Sue Guldin. Once again, I marvel at what a remarkable institution that library is and how helpful and knowledge-able the people who work there are. I know when I walk in with a question, I'll walk out with an answer–with very rare exceptions.

The good folks who run Eddie Brandt's Saturday Matinee–particularly Claire and Donovan–and Dave's Video: The Laser Disc Place have also helped make this book possible. I had to watch many, many movies (not all of them great) while researching and writing *AMC's Great Christmas Movies*, and I almost never came up with a title that either Eddie Brandt's or Dave's couldn't produce for me.

I especially want to thank those people who sat for inter-views for both the AMC special and this book: Peter Billingsley, Chevy Chase, Bob Clark, David Huddleston, Olivia Hussey, June Lockhart, Darren McGavin, Margaret O'Brien, and Jean Shepherd. And the most special of these is my friend and favorite film historian, Jeanine Basinger, Corwin-Fuller Professor of Film Studies at Wesleyan University in Middletown, Connecticut. Jeanine wrote the definitive book on *It's a Wonderful Life* and shared her remarkable knowledge and insight with me on camera and in print. There's no way I would have done a project like this without involving Jeanine in some way. I would go to any lengths, in fact, to have an excuse to get her on the phone to talk movies. Thanks Jeanine. Every time I hear your name, a bell rings...

I also interviewed the great Rosemary Clooney in 1994 for a fortieth anniversary article about *White Christmas* for *Tower Pulse!* magazine. It was one of the great thrills and honors of my life, and I'm delighted to have the chance to go back to that interview for this book.

It was my lucky day when I met Robert Lawe of Fresh

Pictures. A fine director and producer in his own right, Rob edited the AMC special with skill, taste, and more imagination than I had even hoped for. He didn't come to the project with an abiding love for Christmas movies, but he knew how to find the perfect image and how to build the very special mood that we needed. Rob, it was my privilege to work with you.

I also want to thank these friends, advisors, colleagues—and my betters: Richard Bann, Bob Birchard, Kevin Brownlow, Mike and Donna Durrett, Sam Gill, Jere Guldin, Pam Hyatt, Chris Koseluk, Steven Lloyd, David Pierce, Tony Malanowski, Fran Roy, David Shepard, Michael Singer, John Tibbetts, and Lester Wisbrod.

Finally, and most important of all, thanks to...

Charles Dickens, without whom Wilkie Collins and I would have led much poorer lives;

Pete, Molly, and Jake, the Dogs of Christmas Past, Present, and Yet to Come;

And my remarkable wife Claire, the greatest gift I could receive at Christmas or any other time—which, of course, docsn't absolve her from getting me any presents this year.

Preface

*T*HE BOOK YOU ARE HOLDING in your hands represents something new and exciting for American Movie Classics. It is a companion piece to our original special, "The Great Christmas Movies" and it represents an important step for AMC in the world of publishing.

It's a logical step. At American Movie Classics, we are proud to present—all day, every day—some of the best movies ever made. From great musicals, westerns, gangster pictures, and love stories to zany comedies and precious classics of the silent screen, AMC offers a full range of the best the American cinema has to offer.

But just showing you these movies is only part of what we're about. It is also AMC's aim to make our viewers more knowledgeable and enthusiastic about the movies; to augment the fun, drama, and excitement of watching them with fascinating background information about the stars, directors, writers, and photographers; to share behind-the-scenes stories about the productions themselves; to offer you more about the movies we all love.

That's why it was also a logical step to create this book to go along with the special. Actually, *AMC's Great Christmas Movies* is more than simply a companion piece; it is broader in scope, meticulously researched, and written with insight—and,

Natalie Wood, star of the original 1947 version of *Miracle on 34th Street*, grins with Christmas cheer in this publicity photo.

occasionally, a wicked wit. This is a book not only for the devoted and knowledgeable film scholar, but also for the enthusiastic movie buff—because that's just the kind of people who worked on both the special and the book. *AMC's Great Christmas Movies* is so much fun to read because it was written with a sense of fun, excitement, and discovery.

Here at American Movie Classics, we share your passion for the movies. We are concerned with the increasingly important issue of film preservation. To all of us at AMC, the movies are the most important thing—except for you, our viewers. Specials like "The Great Christmas Movies" celebrate our motion picture heritage and the warm, sometimes nostalgic memories that these movies evoke. This book is an important part of that celebration. It is our hope that together they will inspire you to seek out films you've never seen and to look with new eyes at those you're familiar with. That way, your knowledge about the movies grows...and so does your passion for them.

Knowledge. Passion. Bring those qualities to AMC and we'll give them right back to you. And at that place where our enthusiasm meets—movie magic happens. Join us as we celebrate the past and boldly step into the future. But mostly, join us at the movies—on American Movie Classics.

I HAVE WRITTEN a short stack of books over my checkered career. But I think I can safely say that I cried more frequently while writing this one than during the creation of any of the rest (I normally cry reading the royalty statements, which is an entirely different emotional experience). The best Christmas movies are filled with emotion, from moments

✦ ✦ ✦

of sadness and tragedy to scenes of pure triumphant joy. Sentiment may not be absolutely essential to the Christmas movie, but its absence often signals the difference between a *great* Christmas movie and a merely passable one. I choke up when Tootie (Margaret O'Brien) knocks down her snow people in *Meet Me in St. Louis* (1944). I sniffle softly when Sterling Holloway starts to sing "The End of a Perfect Day" in *Remember the Night* (1940). My eyes well up with tears when Mary Steenbergen says "Merry Christmas" to Santa Claus in *One Magic Christmas* (1985). And when Scrooge (Alastair Sim) approaches his nephew's house, to the strains of "Barbara Allen" in *Scrooge* (1951), I don't even try to hold back the sobs.

AMC's Great Christmas Movies, as you can see, is a book that springs directly from my personal enthusiasm for the subject. I love Christmas. Every year, for as long as I've had access to Christmas movies on video tape or laser disc, I've programmed my own little festivals: *Magoo's Christmas Carol* one night, *Scrooged* the next, the great *SCTV* Christmas shows the next, and *The Bishop's Wife* after that. I love the musical *Scrooge* (1970) and *Miracle on 34th Street* (1949) and *A Christmas Story* (1983) and *Black Christmas* (1975). I've even come to have a real affection for some latter-day entries, like *The Santa Clause* (1994) and *The Preacher's Wife* (1997). If a film is touched with that special mixture of humor, sadness, whimsy, and fantasy, chances are it's one of my favorite Christmas movies.

Jeanne Craine and Farley Granger in O. Henry's immortal *The Gift of the Magi* from *O. Henry's Full House* (1952).

An astute observer will note that there have been scores, perhaps hundreds, of Christmas movies made over the past century—far too many for any single book to adequately address. I fully realize that I'm going to hear a lot of "but where was…?" questions. There's not much I can do about that; movies had to be left on my cutting room floor—sometimes for personal reasons, sometimes for logistical ones. Some films I simply couldn't arrange to see or couldn't find any research material on. Others just seemed too peripheral. Except for a brief sidebar, I decided not to even touch television—it's far too vast a can of worms and deserves its own book. And also, save a few unavoidable exceptions, I concentrated almost entirely on American films.

I do regret the absence of Laurel and Hardy's *Babes in Toyland* (1934) and *The Trail of Robin Hood* (1950), a Tru-Color adventure in which Roy Rogers is hot on the trail of Christmas tree bandits. And there are several charming tellings of the Nativity story that didn't make it into the book—*Our Vines Have Tender Grapes* (1945), *Inn of the Sixth Happiness* (1958), *Imitation of Life* (1959), *Let No Man Write My Epitaph* (1960), and *Bright Eyes* (1934).

There are Christmas scenes in countless movies—far too many to address if they didn't have some significant bearing on the nature of the film itself. Although fans might note that Scarlett and Rhett celebrated Christmas in *Gone With the Wind* (1939), that doesn't necessarily make *GWTW* a Christmas movie. The same can be said of that unique film noir *Lady in the Lake* (1946), which is set at Christmas, and Curtis Hanson's great *LA Confidential* (1997), which begins with an extended sequence that becomes known for the rest of the film as "Bloody Christmas."

Even some real Christmas movies had to be discarded for one reason or another, though I would love to have had room for *Beyond Tomorrow* (1940) with its poignant Christmas setting; or *I'll Be Seeing You* (1945), in which a prison parolee (Ginger Rogers) falls in love with a disturbed soldier (Joseph Cotten) over the Christmas holiday; or *Holiday Affair* (1950), a romantic Christmas comedy starring Robert Mitchum and Janet Leigh.

Billy Wilder's cynical comedy *The Apartment* (1960), starring Jack Lemmon, Shirley MacLaine, and Fred MacMurray, takes place at Christmas; and so does at least one lovely scene in Charles Laughton's masterpiece *Night of the Hunter* (1955), with Lillian Gish and Robert Mitchum. Christmas is also part of the background in *Lethal Weapon* (1987), *Die Hard* (1988), *Less Than Zero* (1987), and *The Silent Partner* (1978), none of which could really be considered Christmas movies.

One of the last cuts I made was a chapter on the films based on *The Nutcracker* and Hans Christian Anderson's *The Little Match Girl*. Although both tales–and the movies based upon them–are permeated with Christmas imagery, I finally decided to drop them both because of length and because they just didn't seem integral to this book. One silent American version of *The Little Match Girl* (1928) exists, along with a couple of films "inspired" by it, but the most prominent modern version, starring Keshia Knight Pulliam, was made for television in 1987. The *Nutcracker* ballet has been adapted to the screen in *Nutcracker: The Motion Picture* (1986), *George Balanchine's The Nutcracker* (1993), and the animated *Nutcracker Prince* (1990), but none of them seem like anything but a pale reflection of the spectacular stage productions that every major city offers at Christmas.

That being said, there are many, many Christmas movies discussed in this book–more than enough, I hope, to give you new insight into something you've seen a dozen times or to point you toward something you've never heard of. Despite the title, not all of them are "great." Some, in fact, are just the opposite. But I wanted *AMC's Great Christmas Movies* to reflect the full range of Christmas movies, from genuine masterworks like *It's a Wonderful Life* (1947) to barely tolerable drek like the Mexican import *Santa Claus* (1959). That's why there are chapters on silent films, which have mostly disappeared, and horror films that probably deserve to vanish.

I don't, however, discuss bad Christmas movies with the aim of discouraging you from seeing them. I look at every film in this book as an essential piece of the overall picture. As much as I love *Remember the Night*, there are times when you're just in the mood for *Silent Night, Deadly Night*. The two movies don't even compare in terms of qualities, but that's the great thing about them—there's something for you, no matter how you're feeling at Christmas. What may be junk to you might be a Great Christmas Movie to me.

If I may indulge in a cliche here, I dearly hope that you enjoy reading this book nearly as much as I enjoyed writing it. It has been a singular pleasure to be able to spend so much time with movies that I love so much—even if there was the occasional *Dorm That Dripped Blood* to suffer through. I hope that this will inspire you to seek out some of these movies or revisit some of your old favorites. Maybe this Christmas we'll all be crying together, in the best possible way.

The Christmas party scene from Carroll Ballard's *Nutcracker: The Motion Picture*, performed by the Pacific Northwest Ballet and choreographed by PNB Director Kent Stowell.

Left to Right: George Brent, Joan Blondell, Virginia Field, Randolph Scott, Ann Harding, and George Raft in *Christmas Eve* (1947).

Chapter One

Silent Nights

IN THE December 20, 1913, issue of *The Moving Picture World*, an editor wrote of a relatively new but increasingly important Christmas tradition–Christmas movies. "A generation ago Christmas without the Christmas tree and stereopticon was not only incomplete but lacking in true, attractive and instructive power. We have grown with the times;

not away from these things, but to and with them, in a larger degree. How tremendously the moving picture helps and enlarges the Christmas opportunities. What great pictures are now ready. Never such pictures. The Christmas exhibition can become truly great."

By 1913, of course, Christmas movies had already been around for nearly two decades. There were, indeed, probably more Christmas films produced in those twenty years than in all the years since. Part of the reason for this was the nature of film distribution in the early days of the cinema. In the pre-Hollywood era, distributors had to release new movies every week. Some of the larger companies produced over twenty films every month of the year. Audiences in the early days did not necessarily go to the nickelodeon to see a specific picture; they simply went to the moving pictures, expecting to see a well-rounded program—comedies, melodramas, travelogues. When they returned the next week, or the next night, they expected to see something entirely new and different. Last week's movie to them was like last week's comic strip to us: enjoyable but disposable.

That isn't to say that some pictures didn't achieve individual success—a really popular picture might be remade once or twice within a few months simply because the original negative wore out—but by and large, audiences were focused entirely on the latest, freshest production. This explains how the famous *Passion Play* could be produced by different companies in 1896, 1897, 1900, 1904, and 1907 and be wildly popular every time. People, then as now, would rather see an inferior new version of anything rather than an "old" picture.

Carter De Haven (*left*) gets a good deal on a tree in *Christmas* (1923).

Typical of the way films were made in the very beginning are Biograph's four-part Christmas series from 1897: *The Night Before Christmas*, *Santa Claus Filling Stockings*, *Christmas Morning*, and *Christmas Tree Party*. One set was used for all the pictures, and only a single camera position was used. Nonetheless, audiences were enchanted. A writer for the *Boston Herald* (December 14, 1897) wrote, "The series of Christmas pictures, designed especially for the little folks, are pleasing their elders just as much and are no doubt serving as a reminder to many how happiness can be given at this season by the bestowal of a small present upon a child."

Christmas films in the silent era covered all kinds of themes, of course, but generally fell into these categories: religious films like *The Passion Play*, *From the Manger to the Cross* (1912) or *Cristus* (1915), discussed at more length in chapter 3; movies based on classic literature such as *A Christmas Carol* (1910) or *The Little Match Seller* (1903); fantasies like Georges Melies's *A Christmas Dream* (1901) and *Animated Dolls* (1903); comedies ranging from the Carter De Haven farce *Christmas* (1923) to the classic Laurel and Hardy comedy of reciprocal destruction, *Big Business* (1928); and social or moral films such as *The Street Waif's Christmas* (1908) or *Christmas: The Bad Boy—The Good Girl* (1904).

Although many tend to think of silent films merely as simplistic, innocent fun, the era was filled with hard-hitting, sometimes angry films that called for social reform or exposed various ugly aspects of modern life such as political corruption, drug use, alcoholism, and prostitution.

Because of the spirit of hope, love, and plenty at Christmas time, early filmmakers saw the holiday as the perfect backdrop for the exploration of themes of want, violence, and despair. As the charity official in Dickens's *A Christmas Carol* put it, "At this festive season of the year, Mr. Scrooge, it is more than usually desirable that we should make some slight provision for the poor and destitute, who suffer greatly at the present time. Many thousands are in want of common necessaries; hundreds of thousands are in want of common comforts, sir." The situation was just as true in 1903 as it had been in 1843 when Dickens wrote those words, and moving picture after moving picture set about illustrating the problem and—perhaps—doing something about it.

Mr. and Mrs. Carter De Haven in *Christmas* (1923).

In *The Policeman's Christmas* (1909, Lubin), a policeman surprises a burglar robbing his home. The burglar is an old man who tells the officer that he was stealing toys for his children because he couldn't afford to buy them any. When the policeman learns that this is true, he turns into Santa himself and gives the poor family a nice Christmas.

Another robber is shown mercy in *The Christmas of a Poacher* (1908). Urged on by his sympathetic children, who are willing to give some of their toys to the robber's children, the owner of the estate being robbed has the poacher released "and the entire party proceeds to the home of the unfortunate, where sorrow is converted into joy by the good things to eat, and to entertain, provided by the benefactor." *The Moving Picture World* (December 19, 1908) called this film "a very touching Christmas story."

In the particularly grim *Christmas in Paradise Alley* (1908), an "orphan newsboy, ragged, cold and hungry" helps save a woman being attacked by thugs. When his uncle ("an old humpbacked man") comes along and finds that the boy has been helping others instead of selling papers, he thrashes the boy with his cane. That night the boy dreams that a fairy and Santa Claus come to bring him what he wants for Christmas—"a gun, some new clothes, a watch and some cigarettes"–but he wakes up, which causes his uncle to beat him again. This beating is interrupted by the lady the boy helped earlier, who comes laden with presents. This changes the uncle's point of view, and the lady leaves the bruised and battered child to try on his new clothes.

The Moving Picture World called *Christmas in Paradise Alley* "a realistic piece of work which not only illustrates forcibly the Christmas spirit, but also depicts graphically the hardships of the poor in the tenement districts of the big cities."

Children in peril are a recurring theme in these films–and are nearly always saved by generous strangers (never by their parents). In *A Christmas Letter* (1910), a desperate little girl writes to Santa for help with her sick widowed mother and baby sister. A kind woman on the

From the Manger to the Cross (1912)

street intercepts the letter and rushes to the scene with warm clothes, food, and money. In *The Little Match Seller's Christmas* (1910), based loosely on Hans Christian Anderson's *The Little Match Girl*, a child gazes at the bright Christmas lights in store windows and watches families going to church, all while she is slowly freezing on the street, lighting the matches she is supposed to be selling to give herself a bit of warmth. Just as she is near death, "a gentleman coming out of church has her taken to his home, and the mother is sent for and provided with the means of spending 'a happy Christmas.'"

Hard-luck Christmas stories could be played for laughs,

such as in *The Hoboes' Xmas* (1910) in which some tramps steal some tainted turkeys and get a hilarious case of food poisoning; others were fantasies like *A Christmas Legend* (1910) in which a kindly man, with a sick child, takes home a poor beggar on Christmas Eve. After being fed and treated with care, the old beggar turns into Santa Claus, heals the little girl, then vanishes abruptly.

A strange variation on the theme of helping the poor showed up in *The Christmas Burglars* (1908). Here is the synopsis from *The New York Dramatic Mirror* (January 2, 1909): "A hardened pawnbroker, after a surly refusal to make a loan on a poor woman's coat, discovers a note to Santa Claus, written by the woman's child. He is moved by the pitiful appeals, and with grim humor, enlists the aid of two unmistakable burglars, with whom he breaks into the poor woman's home, mildly chloroforms her and the child and leaves a load of Christmas presents and provisions to surprise them or their return to consciousness."

Universal's *The Jew's Christmas* (1913), starring Phillips Smalley and Lois Weber (who also directed), offered a plot that spoke specifically to the concerns of many immigrants early in the century and told it in a way that would be impossible today. In the film, religious conflict tears a family apart when a father is estranged from his son because he disapproves of the son marrying a Gentile girl. The son is anxious to assimilate into the Christian culture, but the father–stubbornly, according to the film–clings to his Hebrew roots. Only years later when the young couple's child becomes friendly with the old man–who she doesn't realize is her grandfather–does the family reunite. Significantly, this reunion takes place on Christmas night, giving the grandfather a legitimate reason to celebrate the day.

Best known for his fantastic films, Georges Melies's *A Christmas Angel* (1905) was a work of social criticism, in the words of a film catalog, "a grand picture of Pathos and Humour with a Moral." It's about a little girl so lowly that even the other street beggars shun her. As worshippers come from church and run the gauntlet of beggars on the steps, "Poor little Marie holds out her hand timidly," read a catalog description, "but is refused by all, their patience having been worn out by the solicitations of the other beggars. One gentleman who she follows in despair bullies her and strikes her violently. She falls on her knees bleeding."

One of the last surviving frames from a lost *Scrooge* (1923) starring Russell Thorndike.

Stories of Christmas hardship are so numerous in the silent cinema that it is impossible to even list them all, much less discuss them. One single issue of *Nickelodeon* in January 1909 mentions *Slippery Jim's Repentance*, "a dramatic story beginning with the sentence of the criminal to a short term in prison"; *Christmas in Paradise Alley* (discussed above); *The Little Chimney Sweeps*, "the luckless Christmas story of two lads of tender years who receive an abundance of abuse at a time when most children are being happily entertained"; *The Christmas of a Poacher* (also discussed above); and *The Angel of Activity*, "a pathetic Christmas story portraying the hardships of a poor family at the most joyous season of the year."

But perhaps the bleakest film of the period is *A Christmas Eve Tragedy* (1908). A sailor leaves his wife, who grieves for him but soon takes up with another man. When, on Christmas Eve, she spends the night with her new beau, her husband arrives home unexpectedly, beats the man senseless, puts him into his wagon, and backs the wagon—with the horse—over a cliff. "The picture is both suggestive and repulsive," wrote *Variety*'s critic "Sime" in April 1908. "It is as well conceived for children as an interior view of a slaughter house would be."

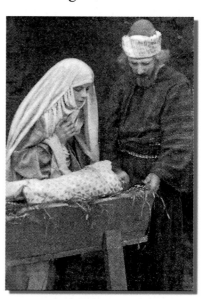

From the Manger to the Cross (1912)

Other Christmas films, of course, concentrated on the happier side of the season. Several were hand-colored or color-tinted after the fashion of the time, but other early Christmas movies were actually photographed in color. Director Theo Frenkel of Great Britain's Natural Colour Kinematograph produced both *The Burglar as Father Christmas* (1911) and *Two Christmas Hampers* (1911). The American Kinemacolor process was used on *A Christmas Spirit* (1912). Kinemacolor claimed to use a double exposure for the first time in this film, something theretofore believed to be impossible with color photography. Melies's *The Christmas Dream* (1901) was even more fanciful and included dissolving effects, tricks, snow scenes, night scenes, ballets, and marches. The climax of the film presented "Santa Claus in His Glory."

Christmas in the silent era was also the perfect setting for "pretty pictures" such as *Reunited by Santa Claus* (1909), in which an estranged family is brought back together by a little girl's Christmas dreams, or *A Merry Christmas and a Happy New Year* (1909), where a put-upon employee, offered a great new job, is able to thumb his nose at his oppressive boss.

Comedies at Christmas ranged from the simplistic–*Sweetheart's Christmas* (1909) shows an increasingly inebriated young man trying to make it to his girlfriend's house, where he is promptly kicked out for being drunk–to the sublime, like Laurel and Hardy's brilliant *Big Business* (1928). In this one, Stan and Ollie play Christmas tree salesmen who have the bad luck to run up against the ill-tempered Jimmy Finlayson. A series of misunderstandings slowly escalates into a minor Armageddon; the boys end up virtually demolishing his house while he rips their car apart. Many writers have found additional humor in the situation by believing that the boys are selling their Christmas trees in the summertime, but as Laurel and Hardy authority Randy Skretvedt writes, "It was actually shot during Christmas week 1928, in the midst of a typically sunny Southern California winter. The studio was eager to get the film finished, before closing on December 29 for installation of sound-recording equipment."

Other silent comedies are too numerous to mention. Mr. and Mrs. Carter de Havens appeared in *Christmas* (1923), photographed by the great Lee Garmes and directed by comedy master Mal St. Clair. In its December 1923 issue, *Photoplay* described the film as "a Merry Christmas. Not to say a riotous one. What with trees, and Santa Claus uniforms and lighted candles and gifts and all the rest of the well known paraphernalia they have plenty of good material for a couple of joyous reels. A tiny colored child helps considerably. And there's a burglar and a goat and a lot of policemen and more darn fun!" Special mention should also be made of Charley Chase's *There Ain't No Santa Claus* (1926), a hilarious mistaken identity

comedy starring one of the greatest and most unjustly ignored of the silent clowns, and *Good Cheer* (1924), an "Our Gang" comedy in which the Gang meets the real Santa Claus—and help capture a band of bootleggers.

The terrible tragedy of the silent period is, of course, that so much of it has vanished with barely a trace. It has

A snow-covered "Our Gang" in *Good Cheer* (1924).

been estimated that up to 90 percent of all films produced before 1930 are gone forever. Many, if not most, of these Christmas titles are permanently a part of Christmas Past, where they can no longer be evaluated or enjoyed. All the more reason to treasure those few survivors. Good or bad, trite or profound, they are singularly precious windows to the way things used to be. Even the worst of them are important. And the best are among the finest things the cinema has given us. If we don't protect these fragile films, and watch them and appreciate them, it's our loss.

Chapter Two

Scrooge Everlasting:
Charles Dickens's *A Christmas Carol*

WHEN Charles Dickens wrote *A Christmas Carol in Prose* in 1843, he did not necessarily intend to create an immortal and beloved work of literature. His aim was far more prosaic: to earn some much-needed money. His serial at the time, *Martin Chuzzlewit*, was being received so poorly that Dickens's publishers had invoked a clause in

his contract to reclaim part of his advance; the author–who supported not only a large family but an impressive group of hangers-on–found himself neck-deep in bills.

There is no greater inspiration than poverty, but even at this low point in Dickens's life, his social concerns nearly outweighed those of his personal life. While researching an article on the education of England's lower-class children–to be given the rather unwieldy title of "An Appeal to the People of England on Behalf of the Poor Man's Child"–Dickens was inspired to work some of his ideas about the poor into a seasonal story. His hope was that he could complete the book in time for the Christmas season. Dickens had *A Christmas Carol in Prose* beautifully designed to increase the book's appeal as the perfect Christmas gift. Four of the illustrations by John Leech were printed in full color. To maximize profits, Dickens decided to publish the book himself.

There wasn't all that much time to get it all done, so Dickens had to get to work in a hurry. In "odd moments of leisure" between installments of *Chuzzlewit*, he wrote the story of miserly Ebenezer Scrooge's redemption in a frenzy–only six weeks passed from the moment he started writing until the day his little book was published.

Scrooge (Reginald Owen) and the cutest of all Ghosts of Christmas Past (Ann Rutherford) in *A Christmas Carol* (1938).

While writing *A Christmas Carol in Prose*, Dickens would walk the streets of London–sometimes up to twenty miles a night–talking to himself and gesturing wildly. The author was as profoundly moved by *A Christmas Carol* as any subsequent reader would ever be, later recalling that he "wept and laughed, and wept again, and excited [myself] in a most extraordinary manner in the composition."

His was, of course, only the first of countless thousands of such responses to his moral tale. Reading it today, or seeing the better motion picture versions, invariably inspires the same mixture of laughter and tears and good-hearted inspiration. Even its first audience accepted the tale eagerly and wholeheartedly. *A Christmas Carol* sold better than even Dickens had dared hope–six thousand copies before the first week was out. Dickens had to reprint twice before the New Year. However, to the author's chagrin, he found himself deeper in debt than ever. *A Christmas Carol* had been so expensive to publish that the income represented only about half the money he needed to break even. Worse, the book was pirated almost immediately, and Dickens ended up spending even more money suing the "penny dreadfuls" that had stolen his work.

In the long run, of course, Dickens was able to reap the rewards of his success. His little book continued to sell at a brisk pace, year after year. During the 1840s, *A Christmas Carol* consistently outsold the Bible. Dickens himself was in constant demand to perform dramatic readings of *A Christmas Carol*; it was the last public reading he ever gave, just weeks before his death in June of 1870.

Scrooge (Reginald Owen) meeting the Ghost of Christmas Future in *A Christmas Carol* (1938).

The full original title of the book is *A Christmas Carol in Prose: Being a Ghost Story of Christmas*. It seems clear that the supernatural elements of the story were what appealed most to Charles Dickens. He was a master of the ghost story, and beings from the Other Side often figured prominently in his novels. However, although there are moments of true terror in *A Christmas Carol*, only some of them come from the clanking of Jacob Marley's chains or the ominous, black-hooded figure of the Ghost of Christmas Yet to Come. The real horrors that Ebenezer Scrooge faces are those of his own making, or those of the society in which he lives. When Scrooge asks sarcastically, "Are there no prisons? Are there no workhouses?" his author knows the answer all too well and knows that the true purpose of his *Christmas Carol* is to make readers see how much needs to be done to improve their world and how little they–like Scrooge–are doing.

The story, of course, has become so well known that it has transcended its origins as a work of fiction and has entered the public consciousness with the life-changing power of scripture. Even those who have never read Dickens's story, or seen any of the movie adaptations, know–as though by instinct–what a "scrooge" is and what "Bah! Humbug!" means.

In brief, *A Christmas Carol* concerns Ebenezer Scrooge, "a squeezing, wrenching, grasping, scraping, clutching, covetous old sinner," a miser who has gradually cut himself off from human warmth in his relentless pursuit of money. He mistreats and underpays his decent and honest accountant, Bob Cratchit, and treats his only living family member, his nephew Fred, with contempt. On Christmas Eve, Scrooge is visited by the ghost of his former partner, Jacob Marley, who warns him to expect three more ghosts over the next three days. The first takes Scrooge on a tour of his own bitter past, the second into the Christmas of the present, and the third into the darkness of an unpromising future. Scrooge is profoundly changed by what he experiences on these three ghostly tours and vows thereafter to be a changed man, keeping the spirit of Christmas and generosity in his heart forever.

This simple and emotional story has proved irresistible to filmmakers over the years, and numerous actors have "Bah! Humbugged!" their way across the screen over the course of this century–actors as distinguished as Seymour Hicks, Albert Finney, Michael Caine, George C. Scott, and Alastair Sim. *A Christmas Carol* has been filmed relatively faithfully several times, but it has also been reincarnated as spoof (*Scrooged* from 1988), musical (*Scrooge* from 1970), cartoon (*Mr. Magoo's Christmas Carol* from 1962 and Disney's *Mickey's Christmas Carol* in 1983), and even pornography (*The Passions of Carol* made in 1975, with Mary Stewart as "Carol Screwge").

Television productions of *A Christmas Carol* are too numerous to mention and date back to at least 1945. If one also counts the number of television series that refer to Dickens's story, or spoof it, the resulting Scrooges would block out the horizon with their numbers.

But as plentiful as movie and television Scrooges have become, many actors have found something profound in the role. Different versions of *A Christmas Carol* take numerous liberties with Dickens's plot and dialog; they even change the time and place of the original story. But the litmus test remains the ability of an actor to create a fully dimensional character, an Ebenezer Scrooge who gradually reveals to us—as it is revealed to him—why Scrooge is the way he and why he is capable of change.

Silent Versions

As NOTED above, Dickens carved out a minor stage career for himself, giving readings of *A Christmas Carol*, and the story was soon adapted for full-scale theatrical productions. But as the nineteenth century wound to a close, a new medium—the moving picture—began to develop and grow. It was this medium that could fully and believably bring the ghostly doings of *A Christmas Carol* to life.

Dickens was among the first authors whose works were adapted for motion pictures. American Mutoscope presented *Death of Nancy Sykes*, an episode from *Oliver Twist*, as early as 1897. In Great Britain in 1898, R. W. Paul produced *Mr. Bumble the Beadle*, also from *Oliver Twist*, and *Mr. Pickwick's Christmas at Wardle's*, a brief episode from *The Pickwick Papers*.

And in November 1901, came the very first cinematic adaptation of *A Christmas Carol–Scrooge: or Marley's Ghost*.

We are not certain who played Scrooge in this first film version, but Dickens scholar Michael Pointer finds

Scrooge (Reginald Owen) meets the ghost of Jacob Marley (Leo C. Carroll) in *A Christmas Carol* (1938).

close similarity between the film's scenario and the then-current play written by J. C. Buckstone and starring Seymour Hicks; Pointer suggests that Hicks himself

Scrooge (Reginald Owen) and the Ghost of Christmas Present (Lionel Braham) in *A Christmas Carol* (1938).

played Scrooge in this very brief movie, which ran 620 feet, or about ten minutes. If this is the case, Hicks has the distinction of playing Scrooge on film more frequently than any other actor, for he also essayed the role in *Scrooge* (1913) and *Scrooge* (1935).

Robert W. Paul publicized *Scrooge: or Marley's Ghost* in an interesting way—he published, as an advertisement, a thorough scenario of the film in the entertainment magazine *The Era*. The film, although quite brief, consisted of twelve tableaux "dissolving and otherwise changing from one to another to form consecutive series and introducing about thirty actors, with special scenery and novel effects."

Scrooge: or Marley's Ghost offers a quite thorough digest of the story. Tableau I takes place at Scrooge's office, where we meet Bob Cratchit, who "gives rise to much laughter in his comical endeavours to warm his hands at the flame of his solitary candle," and Scrooge's nephew, Fred, who tries to "ingratiate himself by offering the old man a pinch of snuff." Fred is, instead, "rudely hustled off, not however before giving Bob a few pleasant words and a small remembrance."

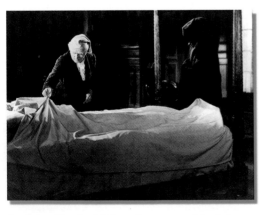

Scrooge (Reginald Owen) sees a grim vision of his own future.

Lionel Braham and Reginald Owen in *A Christmas Carol* (1938).

As the title suggests, there are no Ghosts of Christmases Past, Present, or Yet to Come. Marley and Father Time lead Scrooge on his tour. First Scrooge sees himself as a boy with his sister, then he rather ungallantly breaks off his engagement with his sweetheart by explaining "that he loves not her, but gold."

In the present, Scrooge and Father Time visit the

Albert Finney as the title role in *Scrooge* (1970).

Cratchits and the home of his nephew, Fred. Then Marley takes Scrooge to the graveyard where the old miser is "so moved by terror and by the lessons that he has already received that it is with difficulty that the ghost is able to induce him to look at the solitary gravestone." The stone, of course, bears Scrooge's name.

After this disturbing scene, Marley takes Scrooge back to the Cratchits' home. It is interesting to note that this is the only silent version of *A Christmas Carol* in which we actually witness the death of Tiny Tim. Here, "the poor child lies on a rough couch, tended by his mother," who tenderly covers "the face of the dead child" just as Bob Cratchit "hurries in with a bottle of medicine."

Scrooge's awakening occurs in Tableau XII and he ecstatically loads Bob Cratchit down with food and gifts, has a celebratory glass of wine with nephew Fred, and resolves to keep the spirit of Christmas alive in his heart. *Scrooge: or Marley's Ghost* ends when "the following words flash successively across the screen–'A Merry Christmas and a Happy New Year.'"

Filmmakers did not return to *A Christmas Carol* until 1908 when an American company, Essanay, produced a version one reel in length, approximately 1,000 feet or about fifteen minutes long, composed of ten scenes. This film, starring Thomas Ricketts as Scrooge, is notable for several odd deviations from Dickens. A supernatural beggar follows Scrooge around, inducing guilt early in the film. And Scrooge's nephew Fred is newly married, apparently to the mother of Tiny Tim. Most of the film takes place among the want and squalor of the present, but Scrooge sees visions in the fireplace of his sad past and his unpromising future.

A reformed Scrooge (Albert Finney) goes Christmas shopping in *Scrooge* (1970).

These odd changes aside, *The Moving Picture World* of January 2, 1909, found that it was "impossible to praise this film too highly. It reproduces the story as closely as it is possible to do in a film and the technical excellence of the work cannot be questioned. The photography, the staging and the acting are all of the best, as the story told is always impressive. The scene where the little girl is the only one who will love the old man (!) is touching and brought the tears to more than one pair of eyes in the audience."

In 1910 the Edison Company returned to the subject with Charles Ogle as Scrooge. Ogle, who also played the cinema's first Frankenstein monster in an Edison picture of the same year, plays Scrooge as formal and cold, always grimly turning away from any expression of cheer. As in the first film version, this *Christmas Carol* deviates from the normal lineup of ghosts: Scrooge meets

Alec Guinness as Marley's Ghost and Albert Finney as Ebenezer Scrooge in *Scrooge* (1970).

Marley and "the Spirit of Christmas" as well as a veiled woman who shows him the future. Scrooge learns the errors of his ways without his ever having to leave his room–visions of the past, present, and future simply loom up before him, via double exposures. Unlike nearly all other cinematic Scrooges, Ogle's does not wear a night-gown and cap but remains resolutely in his business clothes for the duration of his nightmare.

The Moving Picture World of January 7, 1911, enthused over *A Christmas Carol*, writing that "it would be difficult to suggest any improvement for this excellent film...[I]t is Dickens's story put into motion pictures and so cleverly reproduced that the characters actually live before one."

The next two versions of *A Christmas Carol* came from Great Britain. The first, *Scrooge*, was released in 1913 and starred Seymour Hicks, who had already devoted much of his professional life to playing the character on stage (and perhaps in the 1901 film). Indeed, the opening title of the film included the words, "As played by Seymour Hicks for over 2000 performances."

This *Scrooge* was based upon the J. C. Buckstone production, which was at the time being performed at London's Coliseum Theater. For such a brief film–two and a half reels–this version is filled with incident that does not come from the Dickens original. Scrooge is more than a miser here–he is actually so tight-fisted that he apparently won't buy new clothes or even launder the ones he has; he goes about dressed in rags, like a beggar. The film invents a new character named Middlemarch, who is meant to inspire Scrooge to charity by his own generous methods. And, once again, Marley is the only ghost to appear to Scrooge–and, in a curious ommission, this Marley wears no chains.

The following year, Charles Rock appeared as Scrooge in another British version of *A Christmas Carol*, directed and adapted by Harold Shaw. This seems to have been a fairly straightforward adaptation of the story; at least this time the full complement of ghosts was on hand to torment Scrooge and to show him the error of his ways.

The major *Christmas Carol* of the teens was *The Right to Be Happy* (1916), a Bluebird Production in which Scrooge was played by Rupert Julian, who also directed. This five-reel feature was most assuredly not filmed in a wintry Dickensian London landscape, as virtually every reviewer noted. *The Motion Picture News* (December 30, 1916) complained that "the players seemed too cold by far. They fairly reveled in mufflers and top-coats, while the California sunshine bathed everything in its rays. Too, the shrubbery in the exteriors showed green and plentiful, while the juvenile players rolled about on grassy knolls as Scrooge shook and shivered his way along the highway."

Unfortunately, *The Right to Be Happy* is a lost film, so we have no way of knowing just how inappropriate the California sunshine was to the story. In all other respects, however, the film seems to have hit the mark. John Cook, who played Bob Cratchit, was singled out by many critics as giving the movie's most delightful performance. "His work was delightfully human," wrote a reviewer for *WID's*, a trade paper (December 21, 1916), "and kept nicely within bounds at all times." *The New York Dramatic Mirror* (December 23, 1916) agreed: "[Cook] is unmistakably a 'Dickens type' and gave a convincing and artistic picture of the wistful, timid little clerk."

Rupert Julian, who would later go on to direct screen classics like *The Phantom of the Opera* (1925), also seems to have been more than satisfactory as Scrooge. He was, according to *The Exhibitor's Trade Review* (December 23, 1916), "immensely effective in the role of the hardened old sinner...and equally so when that gentleman's character undergoes such a singular change over night." The same publication also pronounced *The Right to Be Happy* "one of the most pleasing photoplays produced by the Bluebird artists."

Scrooge Talks!

SEYMOUR HICKS'S *Scrooge* from 1935 is generally considered to be the first sound version of *A Christmas Carol*. But director Hugh Croise and actor Bransby Williams actually brought Ebenezer Scrooge into the talkie era some seven years earlier, in 1928. Their nine-minute-long film, produced by British Sound Film Productions, told the story in the briefest terms and, apparently, with only a single actor. This film is gone now, too, but would be particularly fascinating to see today, both for its treatment of *A Christmas Carol* and for its early achievement in sound film.

In 1933 came a second sound film from England, *A Dickensian Fantasy*. This was another one-man show in which a gentleman, played by Lawrence Hanray, "reads *A Christmas Carol* and dreams characters come to life."

Just as the earliest days of cinema saw a spate of productions based on the works of Charles Dickens, so did

Roger Rees as Fred, Susannah York as Mrs. Cratchit, David Warner as Bob Cratchit, Frank Finlay as Jacob Marley, and George C. Scott as Ebenezer Scrooge in *A Christmas Carol* (1984).

filmmakers and studios of the thirties turn frequently to his works. Nearly every year saw one or more major Dickens productions including *Oliver Twist* (1933), *The Old Curiosity Shop* (1934), *Great Expectations* (1934), *The Mystery of Edwin Drood* (1935), and *David Copperfield* (1935), with W. C. Fields as Micawber–oh, what a Scrooge he might have made!

There were, during this period, two important treatments of *A Christmas Carol*: the aforementioned *Scrooge* (1935), a British production starring Seymour Hicks, and *A Christmas Carol* (1938), the M-G-M feature starring Reginald Owen as Scrooge.

Hicks, of course, had more experience playing the role

than any other actor ever. It is interesting, then, to note that his is among the least satisfying Scrooges on film. Hicks's 1935 Scrooge is as shabby and bent as his 1913 incarnation, who appeared too tight with a penny to even purchase new clothes. While subsequent actors would find some of the bitter humor in the role, Hicks is merely bitter.

This Scrooge is also highly nervous. After seeing Marley's face emerge in the door knocker, Hicks's Scrooge almost comes unglued, jumping and starting at every noise in his apartment, looking fearfully under the bed and behind curtains. The light of his candle catches a hanging suit of clothes, and Scrooge thinks it's a ghost; he is, in fact, the only Scrooge on film with a predisposition to believe in ghosts. The others scoff at Marley at first, insisting that his appearance might be due to indigestion: "There's more of gravy than of grave about you!"

There is literally nothing to the 1935 Marley–he is invisible to us. Hicks plays the entire scene by himself, talking to a blank spot in the room. When Marley leaves us with the parting line, "Look to see me no more," the effect is not quite as ominous as it might be, considering that we haven't seen him in the first place.

Marley's invisibility gives him a lot in common with the other ghosts in this film. The Ghost of Christmas Past appears only as a rather indistinct shape, and the Ghost of Christmas Yet to Come is a mere shadow. The Ghost of Christmas Present is the only one that Scrooge gets a good look at–he's fat and beardless, with a tendency to talk with his mouth full.

Hick's Scrooge lacks a certain dimension as a character, and his visions of Christmases Past, Present, and Future also fall short in life-changing detail. He doesn't go back far enough to see himself as a child or a youth, consequently there is neither a sister Fan nor a Fezziwig. We first see him as a slightly younger version of himself, foreclosing a mortgage on a poor young couple. When his intended, Belle, catches him in this cruel action, she breaks off their engagement. Belle, no spring chicken herself, seems to be about fifty, and Scrooge's later vision of her with a large happy family is not as touching as it might be, simply because the viewer is too distracted by doing the math.

There is at least one more interesting variation in this version of *Scrooge*–it is the only sound film in which we see Tiny Tim die. In Dickens's original story and in virtually all other film versions, we see the Cratchits' reaction to his death, as Bob returns from a visit to his grave ("It would have done you good to see what a green place it is."). But here, a weeping Bob Cratchit sits by his child's body, as Scrooge–photographed with stark, expressionistic lighting–peers helplessly through the window.

Dickensian purists must have scratched their heads at many of *Scrooge*'s deviations, but the film was both a popular and critical success. *Variety* (December 18, 1935) said that *Scrooge* had been "acted with fidelity to character and directed with consummate skill and intelligence" and that it "captured the spirit of the Dickens classic."

Perhaps the most admirable element of Hicks's version is its relentless darkness and morbidity of tone, which does ring quite true to the Dickens original. In contrast, when Hollywood got hold of the story in 1938, casting Reginald Owen as Scrooge, all darkness went out the window. This M-G-M version of *A Christmas Carol* is as bright and cheerful as a Christmas card. It deemphasizes Scrooge's cruelty and the horror of his visions, concentrating instead on the lively antics of his handsome nephew, Fred, and the good-natured sweetness of the Cratchit family's Christmas–which seems quite wondrous enough without the turkey and presents that the reformed Scrooge will later bring. The dirty and dangerous streets of London about which Dickens wrote so vividly are quaint and clean, filled with happy, generous people. In this film, Scrooge seems a complete aberration–a monster with whom the viewer has little in common. And that has everything to do with the actor chosen to play the part.

For several years, Lionel Barrymore had performed the role of Scrooge in a popular annual radio adaptation. It was widely assumed that when a motion picture was produced on the subject, that Barrymore would play the part. Indeed, in the May 23, 1938, issue of *The Hollywood Reporter*, it was announced that he had signed to play Scrooge on film.

But when the cameras started to roll on October 5, 1938 (this for a December 1938 release!), Reginald Owen had been cast as Scrooge. Barrymore had to pull out of the project because of the crippling effects of arthritis and a leg injury that would keep him wheelchair bound for the rest of his life. In the press book for *A Christmas Carol*, the studio claimed that they offered to postpone the filming until Barrymore was better. But supposedly he replied, "If ever the world needed Dickens's message of peace on earth and good will toward men, that time is today." He also added that he heartily approved of the casting of Reginald Owen, saying that Owen not only was a "great actor" but "an Englishman and I can only see an Englishman playing Dickens."

Barrymore went a step further in supporting *A Christmas Carol*: He refrained from performing it on the radio that year so that he wouldn't interfere with the success of the movie, and he appeared in a special preview trailer called *A Fireside Chat with Lionel Barrymore* in which he introduced and endorsed Owen in the role.

The man playing Bob Cratchit was not an Englishman, like Reginald Owen—he was Canadian. But Gene Lockhart's real wife, Kathleen, was indeed British—and she played Mrs. Cratchit in the film. In addition, their twelve year-old daughter June—later a television star (*Lassie* and *Lost In Space*)—made her film debut as one of the Cratchit children.

Nearly all of the critics of the time agreed that M-G-M had made the best of all possible *Christmas Carol*s. *The Hollywood Reporter* (December 9, 1938) called it "a special Christmas treat" and the *Motion Picture Herald* (December 17, 1938) agreed that it was "an extraordinarily special motion picture." Further, the *Herald* assured its readers that this was no "modernized version of the Charles Dickens story, nor a streamlined version, an 'interpretation,' an approximation nor, for that matter, what is commonly referred to as a 'Hollywood' version. With an understanding and appreciation of public attitude seldom matched in the history of art, Mr. Joseph L. Mankiewicz has produced a film which any and all lovers of the Dickens classic may and must relish as a direct, literal, and meticulously authentic transcription of the story from printed page to living screen."

This only goes to show that the *Reporter*'s critic, William R. Weaver, hadn't read the Dickens original in a long time, if ever.

The M-G-M version is warm and homey enough to make for pleasant Christmas viewing, and indeed, it remains among the most popular versions to air on television annually. But as an adaptation of Dickens, it misses both the spirit and the detail of the original. Reginald Owen is one of the film's major problems; his Scrooge is a caricature, peculiarly unthreatening before his transformation and annoyingly and artificially happy after it.

In *Scrooged,* Frank Cross (Bill Murray) receives a friendly visit from his former boss, the late Lew Hayward (John Forsythe).

Seven years after his death on a golf course, Lew Hayward (John Forsythe) returns to the offices of the IBC television network to deliver a warning to Frank Cross (Bill Murray).

The streamlining of the story doesn't help; several unfortunate deviations from Dickens help make Owen less sympathetic and render his redemption unconvincing. Owen's Scrooge has no Belle to love and lose, nor any Christmas party at Fezziwig's to give him an example of the way a kind and benevolent employer treats his workers. Worse, he has his change of heart while with the Ghost of Christmas Present, smiling widely and declaring, "I love Christmas!"—an attitude that renders his bleak foray into the future a bit redundant.

The film also enlarges the role of Scrooge's handsome and charming nephew, Fred, as if to make sure that undue focus wouldn't be placed on so unsympathetic a character as Ebenezer Scrooge. Consequently, there are long periods of the film in which Scrooge seems more of a supporting player than the center of the story, as he should be.

That said, there are moments of great effectiveness and charm in M-G-M's *A Christmas Carol.* The Cratchits spend an unusually pleasant Christmas Day together, with a bit of extra drama added due to the fact that Scrooge has, on Christmas Eve, actually fired Bob Cratchit (he'll be rehired the next day, of course). Terry Kilburn's Tiny Tim is a bit too vivid and borderline maudlin, but the rest of the brood, including young June Lockart, exhibit an easy, natural charm. These assets nearly make up for all of this version's failings, because the Cratchit family provides the story with its most powerful moments of emotion—

Bill Murray is Frank Cross and Alfre Woodard plays Grace Cooley, his ever-patient secretary, in *Scrooged*.

In *Scrooged*, Frank Cross (Bill Murray) discovers a trespasser, Calvin Cooley (Nicholas Phillips), on the set of the IBC television network production of *Scrooge*.

from the glee they exhibit when they get their first look at Mother's pudding to the stoic sadness they show in the aftermath of Tim's death.

The Cast of Characters

EVEN THOUGH the Cratchits always provide the films' greatest moments of warmth and emotion, they are by no means the same Cratchits from movie to movie. Indeed, most of the supporting characters in *A Christmas Carol* change—sometimes subtly—from version to version. Bob Cratchit is a frail, middle-aged father in the 1935 *Scrooge*; a plump, exhuberant, overgrown boy in *A Christmas Carol* from 1938; meek, sad, and hopeful in *Scrooge* from 1951; and optimistic and noble of heart in the 1970 *Scrooge*.

Nephew Fred is hearty, cheerful, and forgiving, always. Fezziwig, Scrooge's old employer, is fat and boisterous and kind-hearted, but in the 1970 version of *Scrooge*, he also has a daughter, Isabel (Belle in the Dickens original), who is the lost love of Ebenezer's life. In other films, Belle is an ethereal beauty. She often goes on to raise a large and happy family, which Scrooge regretfully visits with the Ghost of Christmas Present. But in the Alastair Sim version, Belle is shown to be a spinster, devoting her time to helping others.

Tiny Tim is always frail and sickly, never more so than in the 1984 version starring George C. Scott. This Tim, played by Anthony Walters, is not only genuinely Tiny, but the dark rings around his eyes and his painful movements make it easy to believe that he is not long for the world. Glyn Dearman, in the 1951 *Scrooge*, is rather heartier but unaffected and genuinely endearing—not saccharine at all. Richard Beaumont, Tim to Albert Finney's Scrooge in the 1970 musical, has two moments to shine in that film. The first is when Bob Cratchit (David Collings) is looking in a toy shop window with Tim and his sister. Bob asks the children which toys they like. The little girl points out a particularly lovely doll. Tim, however, says he likes all the toys. After all, he reasons, "You said we can't have none of 'em, so I might as well like them all." Later, at the Cratchits' Christmas feast, they urge Tim to sing a song, and the sad little melody he obliges them with ("The Beautiful Day") is one of the most heart-wrenching moments in any version of the story.

Ebenezer's sister Fan—a rather minor character in the story—grows older and younger depending upon the film. In the 1938 film, she is the child that Dickens describes although, for reasons of their own, the filmmakers changed her name to "Fran." Fan is a young woman in most other versions; and only in the 1951 *Scrooge* does she appear in any scene other than her schoolhouse meeting with young Ebenezer. To his dismay, Scrooge is brought by the Ghost of Christmas Past to her bedside as she is dying and watches his younger self storm angrily out of the room, flashing a look of hatred toward her newborn baby. Only now can he hear her last words, pleading with him to take care of her son.

All actors who have played the ghost of Jacob Marley have had a field day with the role, using his tortured soul as a grand excuse for epic scenery chewing. Alec Guiness in the 1970 musical developed an odd, broken-hipped walk. Frank Finlay's Marley in the 1984 version, with George C. Scott as Scrooge, walks in and unties the kerchief tied around his head, causing his lifeless jaw to drop wide open. In *The Muppet Christmas Carol* (1992) Michael Caine's Scrooge is confronted by not one but two Marleys—the old geezer Muppets who are best known for their incessant heckling.

Of the three ghosts—Past, Present, and Yet to Come—two are generally depicted on film as Dickens described them: the Ghost of Christmas Present is a large, bearded, bare-chested giant who wears a fur-trimmed robe and a wreath of holly and ice on his head. In *A Christmas Carol* (1938) and the musical *Scrooge* (1970), he carries about with him a pitcher filled with the Milk of Human Kindness, which he uses to soften Scrooge's character and to bring bickering, angry people on the street together with gestures of forgiveness. Christmas Present is jolly and boisterous and sometimes bitterly sarcastic; it is he who throws Scrooge's words back in his face, "Are there no prisons? Are there no workhouses?"

The Ghost of Christmas Yet to Come is always an ominous, faceless, speechless, black-robed figure. Even here, though, there are variations. In Disney's *Mickey's Christmas Carol*, the ghost is played by Peg-Leg Pete, a large, angry cat. In the musical *Scrooge*, the ghost eventually reveals its horrifying skull face just before Ebenezer is sent to visit Hell (so far this is the only film version of the story to punish Scrooge *this* much).

However, Dickens's Ghost of Christmas Past is more problematic; it is described by the author as "like a child; yet not so like a child as like an old man." The ghost has long white hair, a wrinkle-free face, and is physically small as though "having receded from view" and seen from a distance. The ghost is a child in *The Muppet Christmas Carol*, an adult woman in the George C. Scott *A Christmas Carol*, an old man in *Scrooge* from 1951, and a sexy young blonde in the 1938 *A Christmas Carol*.

Richard Donner's *Scrooged* (1988) spins even wilder variations on Dickens's characters. *Scrooged* stars Bill Murray as Frank Cross, a television executive ("the youngest president in the history of television") who, as the film opens, is ready to unveil his network Christmas specials. The most notable of these is "The Night the Reindeer Died," a kind of "Santa Claus Meets *Die Hard*" action film in which the North Pole is under siege by terrorists, only to be saved by Lee Majors. But Frank's big gun on Christmas Eve is his live telecast of *Scrooge*, starring Buddy Hackett as Ebenezer Scrooge and gymnast Mary Lou Retton as Tiny Tim.

This hilarious double-Scrooge tale takes a dark turn when Frank's dead boss, Lew Hayward (John Forsythe), arrives to warn the executive that his soul is in danger. Hayward has dropped dead on the golf course seven years earlier and, although badly decomposed, is still dressed for a day of golf. In fact, when a mouse crawls out of a hole

Frank Cross (Bill Murray) hates Christmas until three ghosts visit him. David Johansen plays one of these spirits in *Scrooged*.

Bill Murray portrays a network president who hates Christmas and plans to exploit the holidays for every rating point they're worth in *Scrooged*. Also starring Carol Kane (*right*).

in Hayward's skull, it is followed by a golf ball that has been rattling around up there.

Hayward, the Marley ghost of the film, tells Frank to expect three ghosts, the first of which will arrive the next day at noon. "Tomorrow's bad for me," Frank replies. "How about lunch Thursday? You, me, and the ghost?"

The Ghost of Christmas Past is a demented taxi driver, played by David Johansen; indeed, his hack license reads "Ghost of Christmas Past." Christmas Present is an even more maniacal figure, a sugar plum fairy (Carol Kane) with a violent streak; she not only shows Frank painful scenes but literally causes him agony by constantly, and violently, punching, kicking, and slapping him.

The Ghost of Christmas Yet to Come is a giant robed figure, not unlike those in other Scrooge films—except this one has a television set for a face and a passel of damned souls inside its rib cage.

There are essentially two Bob Cratchits in *Scrooged.* The first is Eliot Loudermilk (Bobcat Goldthwait), a Milquetoast employee of Frank's who is fired on Christmas Eve and whose life begins to degenerate immediately. Within a matter of hours, he has lost his wife and home and has become a drunk. Driven to the end of his rope, he comes back to the network headquarters with a shotgun, out for Frank's blood.

The second and more appropriate Cratchit is Frank's secretery, Grace (Alfre Woodard). At home she has a happy, if poor, brood, including one tiny child, Calvin (Nicholas Phillips), who hasn't spoken a word since his father died a couple of years earlier.

Frank's road to redemption is just like Ebenezer Scrooge's, only when he gets there, it is not altogether clear how seriously the filmmakers intend for us to take it. He interrupts his live broadcast of *Scrooge* and gives a long, rambling speech on what he has learned. The trouble is, the speech is so funny and sarcastic, the question remains—just how reformed and redeemed is he? Only when little Calvin steps up beside him and whispers, "God Bless Us Every One"—Tiny Tim's eternal catch-phrase—is there a moment of genuine emotion.

Bill Murray's Frank Cross is the most unconventional, and funniest, of film Scrooges, but an outstanding array of actors have played the part straight and found the true humanity of the subject. Seymour Hicks and Reginald Owens started off the sound era with two performances that were only partially satisfactory. George C. Scott's 1984 performance, on the other hand, comes much closer to the heart of the character. Scott's Scrooge stubbornly holds on to his "principles" of being a stern businessman and an unsentimental, clear-eyed thinker, even as the three ghosts and their visions gouge deeper chinks in the armor of his spirit. The most sardonic of Scrooges, this one finds the true evil deliciousness of a line like, "If I had my way, every idiot who goes about with 'Merry

Tiny Tim Cratchit (Richard Beaumont) and his father, Bob (David Collings), share a song on Christmas Eve in *Scrooge* (1970).

Christmas' on his lips should be boiled in his own pudding and buried with a stake of holly through his heart!"–he's cackling with devilish glee by the end of it.

On his journey, Scott's Scrooge changes gradually, regresses, softens, hardens again. When at last he collapses in tears at his own graveside and, later, bounces exuberantly on his bed like an ecstatic child, it is easy to believe that he has survived a profound journey and undergone a terrific change.

Albert Finney, in Ronald Neame's elaborate musical version from 1970, is a gnarled and bent old Scrooge, who looks up at the world with suspicion and distaste. Finney's is also, in some ways, the most pitiable of Scrooges; his greed and selfishness have led to a profoundly lonely and bitter existence. If Scott's and Sim's Scrooges have convinced themselves that they are better off as solitary misers, Finney's is keenly aware of the pain of being alone and despised.

Neame's *Scrooge* is graced by several outstanding songs from Leslie Briccuse. One of them, "Happiness," sung by Scrooge's love Isabel (Suzanne Neve), has the haunting quality of a melody by Ralph Vaughan-Williams. And the rousing "Thank You Very Much"–the occasion for two of the film's most elaborate production numbers–received an Academy Award nomination. Notable as the first feature-length version of *A Christmas Carol* in Technicolor and Panavision, this *Scrooge* is also an eye-popping delight.

Although Seymour Hicks portrayed Scrooge as an old man and a *slightly* younger man, Finney is the only actor on film who has actually played both old and young Scrooge. Only thirty-three at the time, he underwent two hours of makeup each day to be transformed into a hunched, wrinkled, balding old man.

Michael Caine's Scrooge is neither so old nor so bitter as Finney's. But then, the film in which he appears–*The Muppet Christmas Carol* (1992)–is far too lighthearted to allow for much in the way of harsh reality. As virtually the only human character in the film, Caine has to maintain his credibility amid a cast composed of wacky frogs, pigs, and bears.

Actually, the film, directed by Brian Henson, son of Muppet creator Jim Henson, does a splendid job of placing the famous characters in appropriate Dickens

June Lockhart Remembers

*M*aking *A Christmas Carol* was a joy. Of course being able to play my mother and father's daughter seemed perfectly natural. It was my first film. I was twelve years old. It was such a genuinely perfect little program, you know. And it was done just as a filler. It ran less than an hour in the theaters when it was released. Joseph L. Mankiewicz, of course, was involved with it. Ed Marin directed it. And I had a lovely experience of being able to be told how the thing worked because of being with my parents.

Interestingly enough I had all my life every Christmas participated in a Christmas dinner presentation of *Christmas Carol*, at our home. We would perform it for the guests afterwards in sort of a concert style, and I'd play Tiny Tim. And our dinner guests would participate, people like C. Aubrey Smith, Walter Kingsford, Dame Mae Whitty, and Leo Carroll, who, of course, played Marley's ghost in [the film]. Many of the people who were in the movie just coincidentally were our dinner guests—and they were all, like my parents, members of the British colony who had come to work in Hollywood. So I was very involved with *Christmas Carol*.

[This item appeared in the Metro-Goldwyn-Mayer in-house publication *Studio News*: "A Christmas plum pudding blazing in brandy after the traditional English style provided Terry Kilburn (Tiny Tim), Gene Lockhart, Kathleen Lockhart and others one of the hardest eating tasks they ever essayed in a picture. The scene was the Yuletide dinner of the Cratchits in Dickens's *A Christmas Carol*. Because the blue flame of the burning pudding would not photograph, the delicacy was coated thick with salt–and the actors had to eat it."]

That was awful. We were supposed to be acting so festive–but I could barely hold my head up long enough to ask the propman, "Could you please set this bowl of turnips in front of somebody else?"

Can you imagine the joy of being able to sit down every year with my grandchildren, have them see their grandmother at the age of twelve, and

A merry Christmas at the Cratchit home in *A Christmas Carol* (1938). June Lockhart is fourth from the left.

then see their great grandparents also in this total classic? Watching it, I'm able to see my parents. I don't know that there's another family in the whole world that can do that with a traditional film like this. It's remarkable.

Working with my parents was a treat always. They were sweet people. It was great humor. Much laughter in the home all the time, by the way. And they were great professionals. It was a craft. At the end of the day they would come home and we would be concerned with dinner. What went on in the house. How I was doing in school. What the dog had done that day. It was not...the best way to put it is that I was raised in–but not of–the business. So that I had lovely advantages of always having my father's guidance when I was working, particularly when I was working with him. And later we did shows together in New York–in the golden age of television we did some things together.

I think that *Christmas Carol* continues to appeal to people as such a classic because it's a lovely story. It's about redemption. It has much of the joy of Christmas, as we know it. Then of course there's that wonderful Victorian Christmas. It wasn't until Albert brought Christmas trees to England that they ever celebrated Christmas in that way, because he was German and introduced the Christmas tree to Great Britain. And, of course, it's all gone on from there, gone on forever. Yes, I think it's just a feel-good movie.

Of course there's been a lot of versions of *Christmas Carol,* but I've got to tell you I think this was probably the best and I think that because of its simplicity; it was done so carefully and with such a tender attention to the truth of Dickens's book story. There were no fancy embellishments or special effects there. It was just a lovely representation of what Dickens wrote.

Of course there are other films that are shown every year at Christmas. It is funny because my father is in so many of them. *Meet John Doe* (1940). He plays the mayor in that. They show *Miracle on 34th Street* (1948) every year. And in that, of course, he played the judge. He was the man who had to decide whether or not this man [Edmund Gwenn] was really Kris Kringle. He was in *Going My Way* (1942) with Bing Crosby. That's shown every Christmas. There are probably others which I forget at this moment. And so when we get around to the Christmas seasons, it's "Hey, grandpa's on again." It's delicious.

Meet Me in St. Louis (1944)

I *loved* doing *Meet Me in St. Louis.* What an extraordinary film that was. We rehearsed the ballroom scene for two months. There was a young lady who was teaching us the waltz. She was red-headed, wonderful, vibrant, exciting–the assistant to the choreographer. And her name was Gwen Verden. That was neat. I enjoyed the film. Of course the costumes were so, so beautiful. I was very amused to find out recently that the petticoat that I wore in it under the ballgown is at Fredricks of Hollywood on display.

The production was very, very long and tedious because Judy would come in around noon. . . .We'd be in makeup at six. Then we'd hang around. She'd come in at noon and then we would all go to lunch, come back, and be dismissed. And this went on day after day after day after day. But when she got there and once she got started working, oh, it was heaven. Just wonderful fun. The dancing scene was lovely. The costumes were by Irene Sharif. And my goodness, I love period clothes. I think dress up is neat. I love to do Westerns for that reason. And when we did scenes at the St. Louis fair in which the lights all went on and it was all–yeah, it was spectacular. We knew it was really a remarkable thing to be part of.

The cast. Oh, Mary Astor. I adored her. I really did. She was so elegant and so beautiful and yet had this lovely earthiness about her, too, when necessary. What a pro. Oh, I admired her very, very much. I'm very, very fond of her. And Margaret O'Brien, of course, was a charming child actress.

Vincente [Minnelli, the director] and Judy on the set seemed terribly professional. And there again, I was oblivious to the fact that they might be falling in love. Although I understand they didn't fall in love until later. It wouldn't have occurred to me to think that there was... I know that Arthur Freed used to come to visit Lucille Bremer for lunch and I thought, oh, isn't that dear of him. He's coming down to have lunch with her in her dressing room. Was I innocent!

roles. Kermit the Frog is Bob Cratchit; his wife is portrayed by Miss Piggy (their children are mixed—the boys are frogs, the girls pigs). *The Muppet Christmas Carol* is clever and at times genuinely hilarious, but by its very nature, it never allows for the true emotion of the story to come through. When Ebenezer Scrooge awakens on that glorious Christmas morning, we feel nothing except the mild pleasure of having experienced an enjoyable film.

At least *The Muppet Christmas Carol* has more imagination and much more of a sense of fun than the entirely lacklustre *Mickey's Christmas Carol* (1983). Produced by the Disney company, this version also populates Dickens's story with famous characters—Scrooge McDuck (actually, better known for his comic book appearances than for movies) plays Scrooge, and Donald Duck is his nephew, Fred. Mickey and Minnie Mouse are the Cratchits, Goofy is Marley's ghost, and Jiminy Cricket is the Ghost of Christmas Past.

This version contains virtually no dialog from Dickens, preferring to substitute jokes, such as when Scrooge is talking about his former partner Marley: "He barely left enough to pay for his funeral—and I had him buried at sea!" By turning its back on the flavor of Dickens (which even *The Muppet Christmas Carol* embraced), *Mickey's Christmas Carol* comes across as perfunctory, emotionless, and shallow. There is some fine animation, as is to be expected from Disney, but little else.

As legendary humbug Ebenezer Scrooge, Michael Caine joins the Muppets in *The Muppet Christmas Carol*, a musical adaptation of the Charles Dickens classic.

Oddly enough, a much finer animated version of the story had already been produced two decades earlier, and by a company from which one would expect far less than from Disney. *Mr. Magoo's Christmas Carol* was produced for broadcast on NBC-TV by UPA (United Productions of America). UPA had pioneered the concept of "limited animation," a more stylized and impressionistic form than the full animation produced by Disney, Warner Bros., and other companies. UPA produced some classics like *Gerald McBoing Boing* and *Mr. Magoo*, but although the concept was fresh and exciting, other studios grasped only that limited animation was cheaper to produce—and that's how Saturday morning cartoons were born.

Mr. Magoo, voiced by actor Jim Backus, was a cranky, nearsighted old man, constantly misinterpreting every-

thing he (almost) sees. He had been appearing in short
films since 1949, but UPA decided that he belonged on
television. *Mr. Magoo's Christmas Carol* in 1962 was his
television debut.

This one-hour special was presented as a show within a
show. As it opens, Magoo is on his way to the theater

Two Christmas icons for the price of one: Scrooge (Albert Finney) dresses as Father Christmas
in *Scrooge* (1970).

where he is starring in *A Christmas Carol*. After a few typical Magoo gags (he walks up to a restaurant and "reads"
the sign "stage door entrance" and walks in), the curtain
rings up on a stage and the play begins.

Surprisingly, the adaptation is quite serious and sincere, with a wonderful and memorable score of songs by
Jule Styne and Bob Merrill. There is genuine warmth in
the Cratchit scenes (Tiny Tim is played–straight–by
Gerald McBoing Boing) and several of the moments in
Christmas Past are quite moving, particularly the scene in
which old Scrooge sings a duet with his childhood self
called "All Alone in the World."

The story was streamlined, naturally—there was no nephew Fred, for instance—but all the essential elements were there; *Mr. Magoo's Christmas Carol* is a real treat, more than worthy of its status as a Christmas TV perennial.

However, the greatest of all Scrooges—the Once and Future Scrooge—remains Alastair Sim, who played the role in 1951's *Scrooge*, directed by Brian Desmond-Hurst (released in the United States under the title *A Christmas Carol*). Sim's is a sardonic Scrooge, snarling out deliciously sarcastic dialogue straight from Dickens but unaccountably left out of most adaptations. Overhearing his nephew Fred and his employee Bob Cratchit exchanging fond Christmas greetings, Scrooge mutters to himself, "There's another fellow, my clerk, with fifteen shillings a week, and a wife and family, talking about a Merry Christmas. I'll retire to Bedlam!" He's also miserly, but believably so. Eating his meager dinner, he asks the waiter for more bread. When Scrooge is informed that there will be an extra charge, he genuinely agonizes over the decision before saying firmly, yet with regret, "No more bread."

Ebenezer Scrooge in happier times. Albert Finney and Suzanne Neve in *Scrooge* (1970).

Sim's Scrooge lives in a London of darkness and squalor; he is everywhere confronted by images of poverty and want. Marley's ghost shows him a freezing woman and child on the street, surrounded by the spirits of those who could have been generous in life but weren't and who now can't "interfere for good." Later, the Ghost of Christmas Present draws back his robe to reveal two gaunt children, Ignorance and Want, telling a shaken Scrooge that these two are the greatest of the world's problems. Because he is shown growing up in this bleak atmosphere while suffering the neglect of his father and the death of his sister, it is not surprising that this Scrooge turned out the way he

did and that it is so difficult for him to alter his life for the
better, even after he recognizes the need to do so. "I'm
too old to change," he tells the Ghost of Christmas
Present in a pleading voice.

Alastair Sim in *Scrooge* (1951).

Christmas Past is given great emotional weight in this version. Watching with pleasure the boisterous Christmas party given by his old employer, Fezziwig, Scrooge is delighted, then overcome and melancholy. When the Ghost of Christmas Past asks him what is the matter, Scrooge says, "I was just thinking I'd like to have a word with my clerk." Revisiting his own kind and loving employer makes him realize how unlike Fezziwig he has become.

Belle, the love of Ebenezer's life, is beautiful and intelligent, and he is genuinely puzzled when she leaves him, complaining to him that he loves gold more than he loves her. Whereas other film versions show her later with a large, happy family in Christmas Present, this Belle sees not to her own happiness but responds to the needs of that ugly and depressing London, devoting her life to caring for the poor and destitute; she lives a life filled with the charity and generosity that Scrooge has ignored and despised.

But the most significant character in Ebenezer's past is his frail sister, Fan. His barely concealed contempt for his nephew Fred is explained by the fact that Fan died while giving him birth. "Just as your mother died giving you birth," the Ghost of Christmas Past points out, "for which your father never forgave you." This detail (not from Dickens) gives enormous dimension to Scrooge, not only in helping to define his embittered character but also in offering him a way back to life by embracing family once again.

Less satisfactory Scrooges are bad for the first part of the film, then abruptly turn good for the climax. The complexity of Sim's portrayal is just another reason his performance is so exceptional and memorable. While Sim's Scrooge dances joyously on his bright Christmas Morning After, like all cinematic Scrooges, there is also a keen sense of melancholy for "all of life's opportunities lost." He mischievously chases his screaming housekeeper down the steps. But when he catches her, his smile turns sad as he comforts her and, in an apologetic voice, says, "No, I haven't lost my senses. I've come to them."

When he approaches his nephew's house, to take him up on the dinner he had previously refused, he hears the folk tune "Barbara Allen" being sung within. It is music

Scrooge (Alastair Sim) and a beardless Ghost of Christmas Present enjoy a visit with the Cratchit family.

that we identify with Fan, and it imbues the scene with a palpable sense of regret. This leads to perhaps the loveliest moment of the film. A sweet-faced little maid takes his coat and hat in the foyer. Scrooge stands at the door, trying to work up the courage to go in. He glances at the maid and she gives him an encouraging smile, perhaps the first smile of kindness he has received in years, and he enters Fred's party. There is more emotion, and more layers of emotion, in this single scene than in the entirety of most other versions of *A Christmas Carol*. This Scrooge is the saddest of all movie adaptations of the Dickens's classic, and Sim's performance is richer, more thoughtful, and more colorful than any other portrayal of Ebenezer Scrooge.

All of the changes, however, are only important to the extent of their impact upon the spiritual and emotional message of the film. The endlessly repeated journey of Ebenezer Scrooge from bitterness, selfishness, greed, and loneliness to generosity, joy, thanksgiving, and love is satisfying on an almost primal level. We all believe that we are capable of change for the better and take comfort and inspiration from the reformation of that "covetous old sinner." Though the details differ slightly from telling to telling, it is Charles Dickens's basic and eternal truth that keeps *A Christmas Carol* and its memorable people and ghosts always vital, ready to live again and forever.

Chapter Three

The First Christmas

HE STORY of the first Christmas, for all the impact it had on the world, was not documented with very much detail. Of the first four books of the New Testament, Matthew, Mark, Luke and John, which tell the story of the life of Jesus Christ, only the first three mention the circumstances of his birth in Bethlehem nearly 2,000 years ago.

✶ ✶ ✶

Of these three, Matthew and Mark mention it almost in passing; the most thorough account comes from St. Luke, and this takes up less than half the chapter, verses 1-20.

So when filmmakers turned to the subject—as they did almost as soon as moving picture cameras existed—they had some indelible images to work with, and a lot of unanswered questions. That didn't seem to matter much. Most of those questions remained unanswered—indeed, unasked—for decades by filmmakers who were content simply to show the star in the East, the humble manger, the mother and child, along with the requisite Three Wise Men and shepherds.

Olivia Hussey, who played the Virgin Mary in Franco Zeffirelli's *Jesus of Nazareth* (1977), says that the sparseness of historical research allowed her to create the character herself. "The good thing is that she's not really a character that you can go read books on," she says. "There was a person called the Virgin Mary, but nobody really knows what she was like–they have nothing to compare her to. So I just played what I

The three wise men western style—John Wayne, Harry Carey Jr., and Pedro Armendariz star in *Three Godfathers* (1948).

felt. The way Franco wanted to me to portray her was as a young peasant girl; innocent and not particularly versed in the Bible or anything spiritual. So I just really did what I felt; I did a lot of meditation and tried to keep it as simple and as uncomplicated as I could–there really wasn't a lot of literature on Mary to read."

Hussey's Mary in *Jesus of Nazareth* is one of the very

few times in which the Holy Virgin is portrayed as a three-
dimensional human being. In nearly all the earlier films,
she is more symbol than person, an ideal straight out of a
religious tapestry. The same can be said for nearly all of
the major players in this drama, from Joseph to the Three
Wise Men to the nameless shepherds. On film, Christ as
an adult has been portrayed in any number of ways, from
troubled youth (*King of Kings*, 1961), to angry revolutionary (*The Day Christ Died*, 1980), to pure, ethereal
goodness (*Intolerance*, 1916). But His birth has rarely
been explored with nearly as much variety or imagination.

The life of Christ was among the earliest of film subjects. The famous *Passion Play of Oberammergau* was
filmed in Bohemia as early as 1896;
the Edison Company replied with its
own version–American made–in
1898. But that was after Rich G.
Hollaman and W. B. Hurd produced
their *Passion Play* in the winter of
1897, filming it on the roof of the
Grand Central Palace Theater in New
York City. Pioneering cinematogra-
pher William "Daddy" Paley photographed the epic, which ran into
some trouble when the Grand Central
Palace's management learned that the
filmmakers were hauling their goats,
camels, horses–and actors–up and
down the building's elevators.

Although these earliest filmed
Passion Plays probably concentrated
on Christ's crucifixion, two other versions covered His whole life. Pathe
Freres of Paris released a hand-colored version in twenty-seven scenes
and twenty separate films in 1904.
This epic production was imported to
the United States by the Kleine

Dorothy McGuire as Mary and Robert Loggia as Joseph in
The Greatest Story Ever Told.

Optical Company, which released in its catalog a detailed
account of how difficult it had been to make and acquire
this *Passion Play*: "The preliminary charges, including
pay for peasant actors, expenses of camera men, and other
incidentals, called for an expenditure of $25,000 before a

single print could be offered for sale. Some years ago Mr. Lubin of Philadelphia offered for sale a set of Passion Play films that were fairly good photographically, but the action was stilted and unnatural, an unforgivable fault in this subject."

The first three parts of the Pathe *Passion Play* covered the birth of Christ, described in the Kleine catalog as the following:

1. *The Annunciation*. The Angel of the Lord appears to Mary, announcing the birth of a child, which shall be called the "Son of God."

2. *The Strange Star*. Led by the light of the strange new star, the three wise men of the East journey to Bethlehem in search of the holy child, whose birth has been foretold to them. They are followed by a large retinue of servants and a train of camels, donkeys, sheep, etc., forming in all an impressive caravan.

3. *The Adoration of the Three Wise Men*. The wise men and the shepherds enter the lowly stable and kneel at the feet of Mary, who holds in her arms the newborn babe. Joseph stands near and watches the touching scene.

Pathe knew a good subject when it saw one. They produced a multipart, color *Life of Christ* in 1907 and followed with another hand-colored film in 1909 called *The Birth of Jesus*. *The Moving Picture World* (December 25, 1909) called the latter "a most appropriate and entertaining film for Christmas. The picture is beautifully colored."

The Lubin version of 1903, about which the Kleine catalog spoke so disparagingly, was released in thirty-one parts of between 100 and 125 feet each. The first three chapters covered the story of the Nativity: *The Annunciation*, *Shepherds Watching Their Flocks by Night*, and *The Birth of Christ*.

As ambitious as the various Passion Play productions were, director Sidney Olcott outdid them all in 1912 when he took cast and crew of Kalem's *From the Manger to the Cross* to Palestine and Egypt to film the story of Christ's life on the very ground where it actually took place.

Written by Gene Gauntier, who also played the Virgin Mary, *From the Manger to the Cross* was a true spectacular at a time when the cinema was still a rather modest entertainment. It was five reels long when the vast majority of films were still only a reel or two in length, and it cost a reputed $100,000—an exorbitant amount at the time. A Kalem ad for the movie claimed that the film required "the services of forty-two skilled actors for the principal parts portrayed, hundreds of natives and camels, and consuming over three months in photographing." In addition, the film boasted some rather startling technical achievements, such as the convincing double exposure employed when Christ walked on the water.

The filmmakers gained the support of H. H. el Husseini, the mayor of Jerusalem, who wrote a letter of testimonial for them on June 15, 1912: "It affords me great pleasure to testify that I have visited the atelier of the American KALEM COMPANY in Jerusalem, and was very much interested in their work which commends itself for being painstaking and thorough to its minutest details. The Company, by the good management of Mr. Sidney Olcott, did not spare any effort to perform the reproduction of the life of Christ on the original spot whenever possible, but in all instances has gathered the best data and material as well as a most competent personnel of artists to attain the highest degree of efficiency."

From the Manger to the Cross was reverent in the extreme and handled its subject with delicacy.

Mary (Dorothy McGuire) in *The Greatest Story Ever Told*.

Nevertheless, it was met with controversy in Great Britain because some felt that the moving picture, by its very nature, was ill-equipped to tell the story of Christ. In Liverpool, on November 26, 1912, a lively debate was held to decide whether the film should be banned. One debater suggested that riots would break out wherever it was shown; another asserted that "he did not think that any actor was capable of representing the Savior on the Cross"; and Mr. Henry Jones, representative of the Noncomformists—there were 80,000 of them—"opposed these pictures being exploited for nothing but money-making purposes." The film was licensed for viewing in Great Britain—which must have been a relief to its predominantly British cast.

Despite the controversy that met its arrival, *From the Manger to the Cross* proved remarkably long-lived. It continued to be circulated to church groups well into the forties. Part of its appeal must have been its versatility. A writer in *The Moving Picture World* (December 20, 1913) suggested that exhibitors didn't necessarily have to show "the Cross" part: "The Kalem film 'From the Manger to the Cross' is wonderfully timely and for this season may be used without the last reel and so keep within the Christmas spirit."

The Star of Bethlehem, also released in 1912, was a more modest Nativity film. It featured a cast of 200 and reportedly cost about $8,000 to produce. Unlike *From the Manger to the Cross*, which is still impressive today, *The Star of Bethlehem* is a tedious affair, whose actors pose in torturous tableaux, as though movement in itself were sacrilegious. Lawrence Marston, a producer for the Thanhouser Company, wrote an article for *The Moving Picture World* (December 24, 1912) on the care he had taken in the production. "The shepherds and the sheep," he wrote, "were posed from a famous painting of that incident. The arrival of Mary and Joseph at the inn is a reproduction of a famous painting. All the manger scenes are exact reproductions of famous paintings. The view of Mary at prayer is a reproduction of Raphael's 'Madonna.'"

But in the same issue, critic W. Stephen Bush didn't seem to care how many paintings the Thanhouser folk had copied. "There is too much melodrama," he wrote. "A constant succession of prayerful and devotional poses and attitudes on the part of the actors is entirely wrong. Piety and devotion do not show themselves that way in real life. Joseph and Mary were human beings and not incarnations of cheap chromos."

Madonna Siobhan McKenna in the role of Mary, Mother of Jesus, in *Kings of Kings*.

In this scene from *Ben-Hur* (1959), Mary (Jose Greci) holds the newborn Christ Child with Joseph (Laurence Payne) seated at her side.

The Italian-made *The Cristus*, filmed in 1915, is relatively routine in its Nativity scene but does manage to offer one twist. The manger here is a free-standing building, round with a peaked, thatched roof. We see Joseph and Mary enter the little hut but don't follow them inside. Suddenly, a bright light emanates through the straw, sending beams in every direction. In this "light of glory," the film says, Christ is born.

In 1926 one of the great epics of the silent era appeared: *Ben-Hur: A Tale of the Christ*, directed by Fred Niblo and starring Ramon Novarro, Francis X. Bushman, and May McAvoy. The early scenes showing the birth of Jesus are not much different in conception than earlier attempts.

Mary (Betty Bronson) is still posed in lovely tableaux and exudes an attitude of quiet grace and purity. But these scenes–indeed, nearly all the scenes that touch upon the life of Christ–were filmed in two-color Technicolor.

Director Fred Niblo objected to the scenes, and so they were directed by Ferdinand Pinney Earle. The film historian Kevin Brownlow called the film's color "as aesthetically offensive as a neon advertisement in a church." But director Niblo actually objected to Bronson as the Virgin Mary, not the color. Kevin Brownlow would not have agreed, "Miss Bronson's exquisite serenity is the sequence's saving grace–but nothing could compete with her shimmering Technicolor halo." (An interesting aside, Myrna Loy was nearly cast as the Virgin, but Irving Thalberg, head of production at M-G-M, insisted on Bronson).

The Nativity did not feature in any major films until the huge epics of the late fifties and early sixties: *Ben-Hur* (1959), *King of Kings* (1961), and *The Greatest Story Ever Told* (1965). There isn't much to any of them except a sense of piety and some beautiful wide-screen compositions. Of them, perhaps the *Ben-Hur* Nativity scene is most memorable, less for what it shows than for how it sounds: Miklos Rozsa's simple and beautiful score is among the most heavenly bits of movie music ever.

Franco Zeffirelli's *Jesus of Nazareth* stands alone in the depiction of the birth of Christ, simply because there are real people involved–people we have already come to know over the course of nearly an hour of the movie. Mary (Olivia Hussey) and Joseph (Yorgo Voyagis) are not remote, idealized panes out of a stained glass window but awed, sometimes frightened, humans, unsure how to react to the strange and wonderful things that are happening to them.

Making the film, according to Olivia Hussey, was also strange, sometimes wonderful, sometimes brutal. "*Jesus of Nazareth*. That took eight months to shoot," she says. "Four months in Morocco, four months in Tunisia. Zeffirelli called me–and he has a great sense of humor; we did *Romeo and Juliet* (1968) together and we're really good friends–he called me out of the blue and said, 'Darling, how would you like to be a virgin again?' That was how he approached me on *Jesus of Nazareth*."

Hussey continues, "It was a great experience. But any time you put a bunch of actors in a hotel for eight months together and nobody gets to leave, it becomes like Peyton Place, you know. It was hard, hard work but very worth it. Hard because of the location. Hard because of the amount of time involved. Hard because sometimes we'd shoot Mary young in the morning, and then the weather would change so unpredictably that I'd have to go put all the old age makeup on in three hours and then we'd get out on the set and the weather would change again and we'd go back. So in the morning I'd be pregnant and young, and in the afternoon I would be old Mary looking up at the cross. It was difficult, especially the crowd scenes. There were just so many extras and nobody spoke the language. It was a very difficult shoot, but a great experience."

Jesus of Nazareth is virtually the only film about Christ that seems to have an aura of earthly reality or that emphasizes Christ's Hebrew background—indeed, it is the only film about Christ that depicts His circumcision. Much of this realism came from the decision to shoot the film on location. Its production cost of $12 million was staggering for what, in America, would be a television miniseries. That money went toward 250 speaking parts, thousands of extras, and several massive sets; one of them, built around an eleventh century fortress at Monastir, cost more than $500,000 and, according to the film's publicists, caused a nationwide shortage of plaster of paris.

Hussey's Virgin Mary is alone among screen Marys in that we actually see her enduring the agonies of childbirth. Filming the scene wasn't quite so bad, Hussey recalls. It was just tedious. "I recall that donkey in the background that wouldn't shut up," she says, "so we had to keep reshooting it. And then the baby—Franco didn't like the way the baby looked, so we had three or four different babies. And that took hours. The actual shooting didn't take a long time. What took a long time was the setting up of the shots and the lighting and getting everything just right. So it was quite easy for me because I got to lay there a lot."

In all previous Nativity scenes, the shepherds and the Wise Men all show up at roughly the same time to worship the newborn Christ. *Jesus of Nazareth*, taking the

At the Joppa Gate: In this scene from *Ben-Hur* (1959), Joseph (Laurence Payne) and Mary (Jose Greci) wait for the census taker at the entrance to Jerusalem as they pause en route to the manger in Bethlehem.

sequence of events from the Gospel of St. Luke, has the shepherds arrive the night of Jesus' birth, and the Three Kings come some time later, on the day of the baby's circumcision. "Yes," says Olivia Hussey, "out of all the films that I've seen on the life the Jesus, this was the one that actually made you feel as though you were there experiencing it."

After the *Jesus of Nazareth* company left the sets in Tunisia, another film crew came along to use them again. But this one wasn't a movie about the life of Jesus—it was about another unfortunate fellow who was born in the manger next-door: *Monty Python's Life of Brian*.

After the British comedy troupe's first feature film, *Monty Python and the Holy Grail* (1975), someone asked member Eric Idle what their next film would be. He jokingly replied, "*Jesus Christ, Lust for Glory*." Actually, that wasn't far from the truth. They agreed that the story of Christ, as told in so many bad epic movies, might offer a great source for satire. However, their focus changed once they actually went to work on the project. "After we'd gotten all the bad jokes out of our system," Idle told *Playboy* (November 19, 1979), "we all went off and did independent research—read books on the period, the Dead Sea scrolls, contemporary histories. I became fascinated with the origins of Jewish monotheism and dug out embarrassing facts about Solomon, for example, who worshipped 400 gods when he died. But what was interesting was that none of us came back with material about Christ himself. There is nothing particularly funny or mockable about what he said. They were just simple, basic truths and moral precepts. But everything that went on in Christ's lifetime gave enormous scope for comedy—the authorities, the people, the churches."

The Pythons created a character named Brian Cohen (Graham Chapman) who just happens to have been born in the next stable over from Christ's, on the same night. The trouble to come in Brian's life is foreshadowed immediately when the Three Kings mistakenly visit him and his stupid, slatternly mother (director Terry Jones). From the moment they come in, the Wise Men feel that something may not be quite right. When Brian's mother learns they are astrologers, she asked him what sign her son is.

times and I'll be back.' So I went outside and peeked through the window. And they did it thinking there was no director there. Oh, and the mothers and fathers—I kept them *miles* away."

The kids start the scene with an introduction—"I'm Joseph and she's Mary and we need to find a room at the inn and that's all you have to know, really"—and end it by singing "Happy Birthday" to the baby Jesus. Father O'Malley and Sister Superior are totally charmed by this genuine expression of the spirit of Christmas, from a group of kids to the greatest Kid of all. So is the viewer. As beautiful and memorable as many of the movie Nativity scenes are, none surpasses this wonderful little scene, performed as it is with perfect joy and innocence—and a wicked sense of humor.

Chapter Four

Jolly Old Saint Nick

S ANTA CLAUS, in one form or another, has been
around for hundreds of years. The real Saint Nicholas,
according to tradition, was born in what is now Turkey in
the fourth century. Historians don't know much about him,
except the many legends that celebrate his penchant for giving
secret gifts. Nicholas left his mark in several ways; he is the patron

saint of children, scholars, virgins, sailors, merchants—and thieves. But because of several tales that have him tossing gold through the windows of the poor and giving gifts
that saved innocents from disaster, he became the model for what we now think of as
Santa Claus.

Saint Nicholas's Feast Day, December 6, was celebrated with the giving of gifts. This
date was about the same time of year when many pagan cultures celebrated the winter
solstice with mistletoe, holly, decorated trees, wassail bowls, and Yule logs. After the
Reformation, when the German Protestant Church gave the Christ Child His own feast
day on December 25, all of these traditions began swirling together to create what we
now call Christmas. In fact, the German term for Christ Child, *Christkindl*, was soon
transformed in English to Kriss Kringle.

Santa (David Huddleston) befriends Joe (Christian Fitzpatrick), a lonely street kid who is skeptical about the true meaning of Christmas, in *Santa Claus: The Movie*.

The Dutch evolved their own version of the gift-giving winter figure and called him Sinter Klaas, a kind of variation on Saint Nicholas. When Dutch settlers began arriving in America in the seventeenth century, they brought this legend with them, and soon enough, Sinter Klaas became Santa Claus.

It wasn't until Clement Moore's 1823 poem "A Visit from Saint Nickolas" (popularly known as "The Night Before Christmas") that Santa Claus took on all the characteristics that we recognize today—chubby and jolly, with a red suit and long white beard, and a flying sleigh drawn by eight reindeer (nine, if you count Rudolph, who didn't join the crew until 1939). Moore's Santa entered houses through the chimney–as opposed to Sinter Klaas, who arrived on horseback–and was referred to as an "elf," which in turn inspired tales of his North Pole workshop where all the toys were created by other elves. The great editorial cartoonist Thomas Nast drew influential portraits of Santa for *Harper's* magazine from the 1860s through the 1880s. These pictures–combined with Clement Moore's description that Santa's stomach "shook when he laughed like a bowl full of jelly"–really completed Santa's image as a fat man in a red suit with white-fur trim.

Many people credit an enormously popular series of Coca-Cola ads in the early thirties with the finalization of Santa's modern image. Here, he was a full-sized human, not an elf. But as delightful as the art in the Coke ads are, the Santa Claus depicted in them is not so different from the one that had already been appearing in the movies for some four decades.

In some of the earliest depictions of Santa Claus, such as *Santa Claus* from 1898, he is very much the old-style Saint Nick. He wears a floor-length robe, with a monklike hood and, most notably, is tall and thin. But by the time he comes around in 1905 for *The Night Before Christmas*, Santa is rotund and dressed in the more familiar suit and stocking cap.

From that point on, the changes in screen Santa Clauses are minimal. He is always bearded–although the beard can range from the neatly trimmed chin of Kris Kringle (Edmund Gwenn) in *Miracle on 34th Street* to the wild chest-length riot of hair on *One Magic Christmas*'s (1985) Santa, Jan Rubes. The sleigh and the reindeer are also fairly interchangeable from film to film, although one reindeer is afraid of heights in *Santa Claus: The Movie* (1985) and another lobbies to become Santa's favorite in *The Santa Clause* (1994).

In the early films, Santa always fits snugly through the chimney–easier to believe in the late nineteenth century when most homes were at least partially heated by fireplaces. But the issue of how a rotund man can get through a tiny chimney begins to rear its ugly head more and more as the decades wear on. The neatest solution is presented in *The Santa Clause,* in which Santa (Tim Allen) actually collapses his body "like Jello" to fit through a chimney of any size. When he reaches the room where the Christmas tree stands, a large fireplace appears, magically and temporarily, in the wall. Allen's Santa is helped by a bag of toys that floats like a balloon when it needs to get Santa somewhere; this bag contains only the toys necessary for one specific house. It is empty when Santa gets back to his sleigh, then full again when he reaches the next house.

Santa (Albert Rabagliatti) and his lawyer, Mr. Whipple (Paul Tripp), enjoy some down time in *The Christmas That Almost Wasn't.*

In *Ernest Saves Christmas* (1988), the bag is filled with magic light. Santa reaches in, takes out a glowing chunk, and it becomes what the good little boy or girl wants it to be. But it only works for Santa. When others, like the dim-bulb Ernest (Jim Varney), try it, the light just becomes useless junk.

Santa movies can really differ in their depiction of Santa's North Pole workshop and in the nature of his helper elves. Elves, usually played by adult midgets or dwarves, are in charge of building the toys under Santa's benign direction. In the great Disney cartoon *Santa's Workshop* (1933), Santa acts as a kind of quality controller, trying out toys and laughing with delight at the fun they offer. In the 1925 two-reeler *Santa Claus*, he is far less enthusiastic and involved, looking at the great mechanical toys and trains with interest, but with nary a ho-ho-ho.

The rather threadbare workshop in *The Christmas That Almost Wasn't* (1966) is run by a mere handful of elves, one human foreman (Mischa Auer), and Mrs. Claus, who is always a pleasant but peripheral character. On the other hand, there are hundreds of elves in the epic *Santa Claus: The Movie.* By the mid-eighties when this film was made, it was considered politically incorrect to use dwarves for these roles, so the elves are full-sized humans—well, Dudley Moore-sized, anyway.

The elves in *The Santa Clause* are played by children, although their characters are hundreds of years old. But perhaps the happiest Santa's workshop of all is in *One Magic Christmas*. There, the toys are made by the spirits of good people who have died and have been rewarded with an eternity in this very special heaven.

THE FIRST Santa movies were content with simply having Old Saint Nick show up and go to work. Films were quite short in the early days–sometimes only a minute or two in length–but audiences were delighted just to see such a magical creature come to life and didn't require

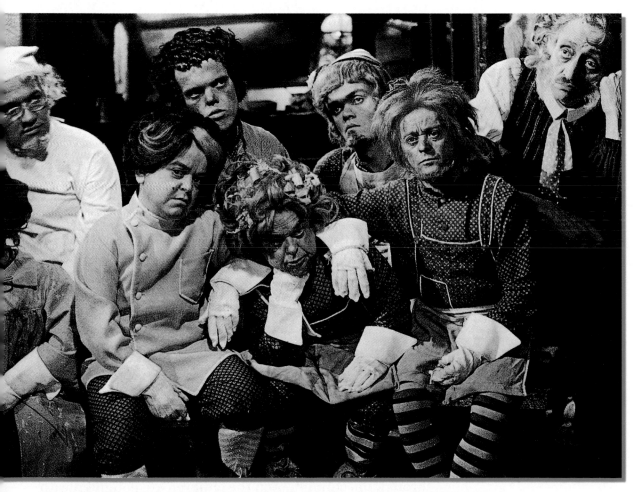

Mischa Auer (*far right*) and some disgruntled elves in *The Christmas That Almost Wasn't*.

very much plot complexity—yet. *Santa Claus* (1899) was described in the Lubin catalog as this: "In this picture you see Santa Claus enter the room from the fireplace and proceed to trim the tree. He then fills the stockings that were previously hung on the mantle by the children. After walking backward and surveying his work, he suddenly darts at the fireplace and disappears up the chimney. This film surprises everyone, and leaves them to wonder how old Kris disappears."

Biograph's *Santa Claus Filling Stockings* (1897) didn't offer much more. From the Biograph catalog: "Old Nick comes down the chimney with his pack of toys on his back, and fills up each stocking to the utmost. When he has finished his work he goes back up the chimney again. Outside through the window, the snow is seen falling and the whole effect is very realistic."

By the time the Edison Company made *Santa Claus' Visit* in 1900, there was a little more to the situation. The scene opens with two little children kneeling at the feet of their mother and saying their prayers. The mother tucks the children snugly in bed and leaves the room. Santa Claus suddenly appears on the roof, just outside the children's bedroom window, and proceeds to enter the chimney, taking with him his bag of presents and a little hand sled for one of the children. He goes down the chimney and suddenly appears in the children's room through the fireplace. He distributes the presents and mysteriously causes the appearance of a Christmas tree laden with gifts. The scene closes with the children waking up and running to the fireplace just a moment too late to catch old Santa Claus by the legs. Santa Claus makes his escape through the chimney, and the children are delighted with the presents that he has left. "This is a remarkably clear

Richard Attenborough is Kriss Kringle in *Miracle on 34th Street* (1994).

picture," stated the Edison catalog, "especially pleasing to children."

The most elaborate Santa Claus film of the silent era came in 1925 from the noted explorer-filmmaker Captain Frank E. Kleinschmidt. Kleinschmidt was known for his arctic documentaries such as *The Alaska-Siberian Expedition* (1912), *Captain F. E. Kleinschmidt's Arctic Hunt* (1914), and *Primitive Love* (1927). He came up with a novel way to use some of his documentary footage for a more commercial purpose by making *Santa Claus*, which was, according to the first title card, "actually filmed in Northern Alaska." In much of the film, a fanciful title card is illustrated by a documentary scene. For example, two children who catch Santa at his work ask him what he does the rest of the year. "I live in the land of Winter," he tells them, "on the rim of the Polar Sea," and his words are illustrated by footage of the arctic. "My borders," he continues, "are guarded by goblins of the deep"–stock footage of walruses–and "The Monarch of the Arctic"–a polar bear–"watchfully patrols my domain."

Santa Claus (David Huddleston) comforts Joe (Christian Fitzpatrick) and tries to assure him that he can stop the evil B.Z. and restore Christmas as everyone knows it in *Santa Claus: The Movie*.

Later, Santa mentions his pal Jack Frost, and we cut to an Eskimo in a weird white-fur suit, smiling and waving at the camera.

Then the film gets a little stranger. Santa describes his "naughty and nice" list to the children and explains how he watches the kids of the world through an enormous telescope at the North Pole. He tells them about a couple of naughty kids–one who tries to steal the cup of coins from a blind beggar and a little rich girl who snubs a poor girl–and after we see the scenes in question, we watch Santa scratch out the offending child's name. No gift this year.

There is, in fact, something genuinely weird about several Santa films. Producer K. Gordon Murray imported a Mexican film, *Santa Claus* (1959; directed by Rene Cardona), to the U. S. in 1960. This brightly colored film is as delightful as it is perplexing. Santa's workshop is run not by elves but by children of all nationalities, and there are some terrific spy-era gadgets that Santa (Joseph Elias Moreno) uses to keep track of who's being naughty and who's being nice.

Judy Cornwell and David Huddleston make a very cuddly Mr. and Mrs. Claus in *Santa Claus: The Movie.*

But there are also decidedly un-Christmasy elements to this Santa Claus. Santa is aided by Merlin—yes, the same one who gave a helping hand to King Arthur. Actually, Saint Nick needs all the help he can get, because he's being attacked by no less than Satan himself, complete with horns and long tail.

In the classic good/bad film *Santa Claus Conquers the Martians* (1964), Santa (John Call) is not bedeviled by Satan but by kidnapper Martians. This low-budget film—which features a young, green-faced Pia Zadora as one of the Martians—is usually regarded as one of the worst films ever made, but its good-natured silliness, intended for the consumption of young children only, is actually quite infectious. It's a film you can laugh at, or with, or both.

At least John Call's Santa fills the bill—he's jolly, fat, and generous, constantly puffing on a pipe and eager to give a good Christmas to the children of Mars, just as he always has to the kids on Earth. The film is mindless in both the best and worst senses of the term, but this is a Santa for whom any kid would leave milk and cookies.

In contrast, there is nothing jolly about the Santa Claus in Rossano Brazzi's oddball musical fantasy, *The Christmas That Almost Wasn't* (1966). This Saint Nick (Alberto Rabagliatti) is so dour and slumped with depression that he walks the street at night in a trench coat and wide-brimmed hat—film noir style. As he explains to attorney Sam Whipple (Paul Tripp), a miserly old crab named Phineas T. Prune (Rossano Brazzi) has recently purchased the North Pole and wants to evict Santa for nonpayment of rent.

An evil toy manufacturer (John Lithgow) influences an inventive elf (Dudley Moore) in *Santa Claus: The Movie.*

Prune is a mustache-twirling villain straight out of

stage melodrama—he seems to be playing for laughs, but it's hard to tell since this film is so relentlessly humorless. Prune, who not only hates kids but denies that he ever was one himself, wants to put Santa out of business because he can't stand the idea of children anywhere receiving gifts on Christmas Eve.

Meanwhile, Santa has his own issues with children. He and Whipple attempt to raise money to pay the rent by taking a job in a local department store in a town that

Dueling anagrams in *Santa Claus* (1959).

apparently has never before conceived of the idea of putting Santa Claus in the toy department for children to visit. The real Santa would seem to be the perfect candidate to act as a department store Santa (see *Miracle on 34th*

Street), but he's terrified at the thought of meeting children when they're actually awake. After a bit of tutoring on how to talk to children and—gasp!—how to say "Ho-ho-ho!" he finds that he gets along with the kids just fine.

Unfortunately, Prune buys the department store and promptly fires Santa—at 10 PM on Christmas Eve, only two hours before the rent is due and Santa is to be evicted. When the kids of the town hear of Santa's financial troubles, they come rushing through the streets in their pajamas, piggy banks in hand, offering their money to help bail him out. He is able to pay off the rent just in the (Saint) nick of time and still make his rounds, with Mr. Whipple and Mrs. Claus on hand to help out. Their last stop is at Mr. Prune's dank and dusty place. It seems that the elf foreman, Jonathan (Mischa Auer), has found an old letter from five-year-old Phineas Prune asking for a sailboat. The letter had been misplaced, so Santa had never visited the increasingly bitter boy. But now Prune has his sailboat and regrets all the Christmases that he has missed.

In the K. Gordon Murray Mexican import *Santa Claus* (1959), elves don't make the toys—children from all nations do.

The ending of the film is a bizarre variation on the finale of *A Christmas Carol*. In that story, everyone is delighted to meet the new reformed Scrooge. But here, Prune's change of heart seems to disturb and disorient everyone. He chases children around trying to hug them or give them a gift, and they run screaming from him. He finally tackles one unfortunate little lad and forces the sailboat on him. The last we see of this child, his face holds something between a smile and a grimace.

As the film ends, these words appear on the screen: "All characters in this story are fictitious—except Santa Claus."

In the early eighties it was announced that producers Alexander and Ilya Salkind, who had given us such box office hits as *Superman* (1978) and *Supergirl* (1984), announced that they were bringing another flying legend to the screen—Santa Claus.

Santa Claus: The Movie (1985), in fact, would turn out to be one of the most ambitious and expensive films ever made, finally weighing in at a reported budget of $50 million. "It had to cost that much," Ilya Salkind told a reporter at the time. "It was more complicated than the *Superman* films. This time we had to get eight reindeer to fly." At least $2 million of that budget went to building Santa's North Pole workshop, a huge structure, all wood and fabric, that resembles an epic-sized ski lodge. More

money was spent on location work that included a trip to the Arctic Circle. And still more went to securing the film's only big name, Dudley Moore, as Santa's main elf, Patch. "I'm the go-ahead elf up at the Pole," Moore said at the time. "I want to modernize the old workshop. There's a disagreement. I leave and go to New York. I get manipulated by an unscrupulous toy manufacturer, B. Z. (John Lithgow), into helping him in his dastardly plot against Santa."

David Huddleston was cast as Santa Claus. A great character actor with a rotund figure and a broad smile, Huddleston seemed

Santa (Joseph Elias Moreno) guides some very lifelike reindeer in *Santa Claus* (1959)—and they're *still* more animated than this movie.

born to play the role. "That was a lot of money to spend on a picture," he says, "but you see they had an animatronic unit. They had real reindeer that I had to drive. And of course they had to train them for a year or two before we started. And they had the miniature units. Jeannot Szwarc, who was the director, handled all of that marvelously. I mean it all came together. It was quite a feat."

Huddleston says today that he looks back on the production "with great happiness and fondness. The British crews that worked on this picture were so accommodating, so wonderful—it was just great." But he does remember aspects that weren't so pleasant. "The aerial scenes were the parts I most disliked," he recalls, "because I had to be in the sleigh way up in the air with a blue screen behind me. It was very nerve-wracking; some of those things were difficult, but we got it done."

Santa Claus was the first film to explore how Saint Nick got the job in the first place. Screenwriter David Newman

A few scenes from David Horsley's *Santa Claus* (1916).

said, "The Santa we know in America comes out of the poem 'A Visit from Saint Nickolas.' But while it's a given that he lives in the North Pole and makes toys for good boys and girls, there's very little that's known about him. I had to work backwards and imagine how somebody would get to be this man."

He created characters Claus and Anya, a woodcutter and his wife who are lost in a blizzard in "the ninth or tenth century." They freeze to death in a blizzard and are transported to the North Pole, where they are offered the chance of eternal life, delivering toys around the world at Christmas. Indeed, the early scenes of Santa Claus are truly magical, including his first sight of the toy workshop and the first time he puts on the suit and flies off in his sleigh. It is only when the bad-toymaker plot kicks in for the film's second half that things get sticky.

When *Santa Claus* was released in November 1985, the critics were naughty indeed. "It has the manner of a listless musical without any production numbers," wrote Vincent Canby in *The New York Times* (November 27, 1985). "From the appearance of the toys that the elves turn out, this Santa's workshop must be the world's largest purchaser of low-grade plywood. Even the sleigh flying scenes aren't great."

David Edelstein of the *Village Voice* (December 3, 1985) wrote, "It's not even as much fun as *Santa Claus Conquers the Martians*."

There are several other Santa Claus movies discussed at some length elsewhere in this book—*Miracle on 34th Street*, *One Magic Christmas*, *Ernest Saves Christmas*, and *The Santa Clause*. Some are terrific, others awful, but each carries with it the residual good will that accompanies the jolly fat man everywhere he goes—even if he occasionally goes into bad movies. These movies offer variations on Santa, his elves, his workshop, and his methods. But no matter how he changes, in no matter what unworthy situations he finds himself, Santa is always Santa; we might not believe in the scripts or acting or direction of these Santa movies, but we always believe in him.

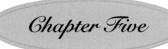

Chapter Five

Have Yourself a
Scary Little Christmas

*I think it's a little spooky when you see a film and you
see Christmas trees and things like murders going on.*

OLIVIA HUSSEY, on *Black Christmas*

ON THE SURFACE, nothing seems more antithetical to
the idea of Christmas than the horror film. There's
something disturbingly incongruous about mad slashers
and serial killers leaving a gory trail at this most festive season.
But numerous filmmakers have glimpsed the terror beneath
the tinsel and have unleashed a savage horde of maniacs onto

✳ ✳ ✳

who knows how many unsuspecting college students and department store
Santas.

Perhaps, though, these hatchet-wielding maniacs and Elves from Hell don't spring
entirely from left field. Who among us, trapped in the midst of a frenetic mob in a
department store or wallowing in holiday-infested family angst, hasn't fantasized
about picking up a machete and slashing a gory swath through the public at large?

The darkness at the heart of the Christmas season is very real and has been explored
on film many times, from the ghostly visions of Ebenezer Scrooge to the near suicidal

angst of George Bailey in *It's a Wonderful Life*. But these movies—though filled with the terrors of the night—always lead to a bright, shining Christmas morning of forgiveness, hope, and happiness.

There is no such welcoming Christmas Day in the horror films. In these movies, nothing is ever resolved, and the terror continues beyond the closing credits. When the berserk Santa of *Silent Night, Deadly Night* is destroyed, another is there to take his place. And just when we know who the killer is in *Black Christmas*, and we heave a sigh of relief for the film's lone survivor, the phone rings, proving that we really know nothing at all.

Margot Kidder as a foul-mouthed co-ed in *Black Christmas*.

Christmas horror movies divide neatly into two categories: those in which the Christmas background is incidental, a kind of ironic decoration behind the mayhem, and those in which Christmas themes are integral to the plot. One of the best films in the horror genre, Bob Clark's *Black Christmas* (1974), falls into the first category. The girls, who are being killed off one by one as their sorority house is shut down for the holidays, could just as easily have been picked off at spring break or just before summer vacation. Christmas, in this case, is the setting but not the theme.

In the other category, we have *Silent Night, Deadly Night* (1984). In this movie, the disturbed Bill wanders about dressed as Santa, pronouncing people "Naughty!" before he axes or hacks or impales or shoots them. He has serious issues with Christmas.

At least Billy roams around town, looking for naughty people to punish; it shows he has a little initiative. The far more blasé maniacal killer in *Silent Night, Bloody Night* (1973) doesn't have to waste much time stalking his victims; he simply calls them on the phone, tells them to come up to his house—the house that they all have feared and avoided for years—and voila! they fall right into his lap, offering their necks for a quick chop of the hatchet. Perhaps that's one reason this Christmas horror film didn't inspire much admiration, even among rabid fans of the genre; we like our slashers to have a little ingenuity, some otherworldy powers. When a demented killer simply phones for a victim, as though he's ordering a pizza, the audience senses that he really isn't giving the best that's in him. And once a slasher loses the respect of his audience, he has nothing.

Silent Night, Bloody Night was filmed on a budget so low the filmmakers couldn't even afford logic or characterization. Here's the story in a nutshell, where it belongs: There's a magnificent house on the edge of town. It's fully furnished and filled with rare antiques and dark secrets. Everyone who lives in the area regards it with the raised eyebrow of suspicion. They avoid the place, wouldn't go there on a bet. In fact, the city fathers, such as they are, have been trying to buy the house for years, just so they can tear it down and be done with it.

Finally, they get their chance. A lawyer (Patrick O'Neal) arrives, meets with the mayor (Walter Abel), the editor of the town paper (John Carradine), the sheriff, and the local telephone operator (I *said*, such as they are), and tells them that the owner will sell for fifty grand in cash. He then announces that he and his toothsome, vaguely European girlfriend (Astrid Heerin) intend to spend the night (Christmas Eve) in the place and finish the real estate transaction later. The mayor and everybody strongly suggest that he might be better off in one of the local motels, but you know lawyers.

Well, the first couple of people who arrive at the old house are killed by an ax-wielding maniac. Then the maniac calls someone else and invites them up; they arrive and get axed. And so on and so on. Meanwhile, the mayor's daughter (Mary Woronov) meets the real owner of the house (James Patterson), and they drive aimlessly from place to place until finally even *they* go to the house where they learn– via a very long and sepia-toned flashback– the truth behind some of those dark secrets I was telling you about. (Without spoiling the movie for those who haven't had the pleasure, I'll just say that the truth involves incest, an insane asylum, and the bloody massacre of a bunch of drunken doctors. I swear.) After they learn these things, more people die. The End.

As a Christmas horror film, *Silent Night, Bloody Night* just slips in under the wire. It's set on Christmas Eve, and the musical score occasionally launches into a somber, minor-key rendition of "Silent Night," but that's about as far as the connection goes. If you saw the film under either of its other titles–*Death House* or *Night of the Dark Full Moon*–you wouldn't be missing a thing.

The Dorm That Dripped Blood (1981) has a marginally more authentic tie to the season, but it still belongs to the category of films in which Christmas serves as background but isn't a necessary plot point. *Dorm* is about a group of do-gooder college kids who devote their two-week Christmas break to help prepare an old dormitory to be torn down. They have quite a few items on their "to do" list–they have to inventory everything, arrange to sell some of the old furniture, and get hacked to death in various and only slightly believable ways. All that can make for a hectic fortnight.

The maniacal killer in *The Dorm That Dripped Blood* operates strictly by the Slasher Handbook. He murders in an orderly girl-boy-girl lineup, he always shares his point of view with us via a roaming subjective camera, he never kills two people in exactly the same way, although that would be much easier and faster, and he holds off killing the last victim for a long, long time so that he can explain why he's been doing all this gruesome stuff.

The killer also thoughtfully wears the same kinds of tennis shoes and flared jeans as every red herring who comes flitting through this movie. And this movie is stuffed to the gills with red herrings–suspicious characters wander in and out of the plot as though they're as dazed and puzzled as we are.

The victims also behave according to code. Alone in this huge, empty building, afraid of a strange drifter type who may be lurking about, they decide to split up to look for him. They're constantly saying things like, "You go up to the second floor–I'll see if there's anything in the basement." Of course, no one deserves to be boiled alive in a huge pressure cooker, but when it happens in this movie, you have to accept it with a fatalistic shrug. Sure, it may be a failure of our educational system, but any college student as stupid as these really have no better future in store.

And speaking of our educational system, *The Dorm That Dripped Blood* was produced as a student project on 16mm film at a budget of, depending upon who you believe, $90,000 or $150,000 by UCLA film students Jeff

Obrow, Stephen Carpenter, and Stacey Giachino. Obrow said the inspiration came from a Christmas vacation when the three were really stuck in the dorm. "It was so scary and empty," he said, "we thought, 'Wouldn't this make a great horror film?'" And maybe it would.

John Saxon is concerned about a Christmas slasher in *Black Christmas*.

The filmmakers studied every horror film they could get their hands on, and since the audience for such films really seemed to expect buckets of gore, they "decided to give them what they had come to see." Oddly, given that decision, *The Dorm That Dripped Blood* doesn't exactly drip blood, not much, anyway. There's a relatively high body count, but nearly all the killings take place discreetly offscreen. (If only more of the film had taken place offscreen.)

Originally titled *Death Dorm* and then renamed *Pranks*, the film got some marginal theatrical play in 1983; it is safe to say, however, that the great majority of

Smothered in plastic—One of the early victims in *Black Christmas* is Lynne Griffin, shown here as the killer leaves her in the attic of a sorority house.

viewers have experienced *The Dorm That Dripped Blood* on video or cable TV. *Variety*, which finally got around to reviewing the film on April 4, 1984, called it "low-budget, low-interest...as with most pictures of this type, film suffers from the fact that *it is not about anything* [italics theirs]."

A much better Christmas horror film–in fact, the classic of the genre–is also set in a dormitory over Christmas vacation. But in Bob Clark's *Black Christmas*, the dorm has a little style (it looks like a gothic mansion), and the students who live there are vivid, three-dimensional characters, not just a roster of victims.

A sorority house at a Canadian college is slowly being shut down for the holidays. Only three of the residents– Jess (Olivia Hussey), Barb (Margot Kidder), and Phyl (Andrea Martin)–are planning to stay on campus until the next semester starts. All the rest are packing up and leaving, one by one.

The dormitory has been plagued with disturbingly strange phone calls by a gasping, wheezing creature who calls himself "Billy." What we know–and what the girls in the dorm do not–is that Billy is also stalking and murdering the residents, starting with Claire (Lynne Griffin), whom he smothers and keeps in the attic in a rocking chair, a plastic bag pulled tightly over her head.

Jess is having problems on other fronts as well. Pregnant, she has told her possessive boyfriend Peter (Kier Dullea) that she intends to have an abortion. He responds furiously and threatens dark revenge if she does such a thing.

Director Clark, who went on to make *A Christmas Story* (1984), says he was first attracted to the project as a professional stepping stone: "At that time," he says, "I felt that the best way to break through [as a director] with any kind of autonomy and control was to do a horror film. I didn't particularly want to do anything grisly. It wasn't to my taste. And I thought it would be a novel idea. I didn't know of any horror film set against the background of Christmas. I thought the contrast of those two images could be something quite chilling. In fact, I don't think the original story was set at Christmas. We added that element."

Although nearly all the victims in this film are women, *Black Christmas* is refreshing in that it does not subscribe to the "they deserved it" ethos of so many subsequent slasher films; the women are simply in the wrong place at the wrong time. "I was very conscious of that," Clark says. "Because they were women victims, I did not want it to seem as if they were being punished for something. They did not deserve what happened; they were quite normal, attractive people. I just wanted to make sure that the *murderer* was the villain and in no way were the victims to be the villains. They were to be the victims."

Olivia Hussey came to the film at a time when she was still best known as Juliet in Franco Zeffirelli's influential 1968 version of *Romeo and Juliet*. "I'd never done a horror film," she says. "I'd never done something with murders and gore, and I think that was my main attraction to *Black Christmas*. After working in *Romeo and Juliet*, I was always cast in these romantic roles, you know, and I wanted to do something horrible."

Black Christmas is nerve-wracking and disturbing, but is not a gore film per se. Even the most graphic murder in the film, in which one of the sorority sisters is stabbed with the long horn of a glass unicorn (as carolers sing away at the front door), seems downright prim beside the buckets-of-blood filmmaking to come in the *Friday the Thirteenth* and *Nightmare on Elm Street* series.

Clark says with a smile, "Ah, the sequence [with] the unicorn. I've always remembered it fondly. I think it was a fresh way to film that kind of scene; I tried to make everything in the killings and the settings as beautiful as possible. The Christmas music. These wonderful little children out singing this glorious song, and these glass unicorns that he used as the weapon, and just the flow of that sequence cutting back and forth to those idealistic little children's faces singing the song. It was somehow both beautiful and horrifying at the same time. I don't find the expending of blood particularly frightening. It's horrifying. It's gruesome but it's not frightening. It's what precedes it that is the most fearful thing to me. I did show the results of the murders, but no blood spurting. No limbs. No–that was gentler times. It wasn't long after that, that it started to change."

Like most mystery films, *Black Christmas* uses a red herring–a character that we in the audience are certain is the killer but who turns out not to be. Olivia Hussey recalls that even those making the film were not quite sure who the real killer would turn out to be. "In fact," she says, "as I recall, Bob shot two different endings. One, in which my boyfriend turns out to be the maniac, and one in which he isn't."

In the released film, the ending is ambiguous, leaving more questions than answers. "Life is like that," Bob Clark says. "Lots of loose ends. And I'm not trying to be metaphorical or particularly pretentious about it. But just the idea of that phone ringing at the end seemed very chilling to me. I later almost regretted it because Olivia Hussey did play a wonderful character. I admired this young lady. She was exceptional. Someone said to me once, 'Well, she did the stupid thing that they always do in these stupid movies. She ran back in the house.' I said, 'That's amazing that you would think that was stupid. She had two girlfriends upstairs who might be murdered. She took the time to get a weapon—I thought it was quite heroic. This is a person who couldn't leave someone to die when she could have gotten away.' So Jess was such a terrific character, later it was uncomfortable for me to think that she might not survive. Fortunately the movie doesn't say one way or another. If I'd ever done the sequel, I would have made damn sure she did survive. She deserved it."

The heroine (Julie Austin) of *Elves* (1989) doesn't much deserve to survive the improbable horrors inflicted upon her. She starts the movie off by taking her two airhead friends into the woods (the woods her grandfather has *forbidden* her to enter!) to hold a secret ceremony as "The Sisters of Anti-Christmas." Now, that suggests a bad attitude right there. Further, she has with her one of Gramps's secret books and uses it to start summoning up evil powers and whatnot. The deed really isn't done until she cuts her hand and bleeds into the earth—that blood resurrects a weird, ugly little being that we'll call, for lack of a better term, the Elf.

The Elf follows her home and kind of attacks her little brother, but no one much bothers about it. Her mother (Deanna Lund) is just too rigidly evil to care about Elf attacks. She hates her daughter, and this hatred manifests itself in, for no apparent reason, drowning the cat in the toilet.

Meanwhile, our heroine works at a department store where the cocaine-sniffing Santa has just been castrated and murdered by the Elf. This causes some concern

starts "punishing" people left and right, growling "Naughty!" as he impales a teenage girl on the antlers of a mounted deer or plants a hammer in his boss's head.

You can't really blame Billy. At the Christmas party, his boss poured him a drink and said, "By the time I'm through with you, you'll think you *are* Santa!" Then later the boss says, "You know what Santa does on Christmas Eve, don't you?" Billy knows, indeed. "Go get 'em!" And he does.

At the end of the film, when Billy is no longer with us, his little brother at the orphanage looks at the Mother Superior in a sinister way and says, "Naughty!" Here we go again.

Silent Night, Deadly Night inspired a landslide of outrage, and not just from movie critics. In fact, the ads themselves were considered as dangerous as the movie. One angry mother said, "I have an impressionable three-year-old. On Christmas Eve he expects Santa to come down the chimney with gifts. In this ad a man in a Santa suit comes with an ax. I can't imagine a child seeing that and not being frightened." In less time than it takes to say picket line, people were organizing protests, circulating petitions, and printing placards with slogans such as "Deck the Halls with Holly, Not Bodies." One theater in the Bronx was picketed by 100 carol-singing protesters.

He knows when you've been naughty...Brian Wilson in *Silent Night, Deadly Night*.

Although producer Ira Barmak sympathized with the parents' point of view ("We're not sleazy, cigar-chewing profiteers," he claimed), he didn't apologize for the use of Santa in such a bloody context. "Santa is not a religious figure," Barmak said, "he's a mythic character. I didn't deliberately ride roughshod over that sensitivity and I didn't anticipate the objection to it."

Nevertheless, protests met the film in Brooklyn, Chicago, and Milwaukee, and the uproar continued until Tri-Star pulled the movie from theaters. It was bought back by its producers and—in a twist more surprising than anything in the film—a sequel to *Silent Night, Deadly Night* was in the works in no time.

Actually, over a decade prior to *Silent Night, Deadly Night*, the first brutally murderous Santa appeared on film in a British feature called *Tales from the Crypt* (1972). Starring Joan Collins, Sir Ralph Richardson, Peter Cushing, and Richard Greene, *Tales from the Crypt* was adapted from the wonderfully gory and hilarious EC horror comics of the early fifties. In the feature, a group of people touring the catacombs under a monastery find themselves trapped in a chamber with a mysterious robed figure (Richardson). One by one they flash back to horrible stories that all seem to end in their deaths. Finally, it dawns upon them that they aren't in a monastery at all but in, well, you know...

The first story, "...And All through the House" is a heartwarming Christmas tale of murder avenged by cruel fate. Based on a story that originally appeared in the Feb./Mar. 1954 EC comic *Vault of Horror*, "...And All through the House" begins as a wife (Joan Collins) gives her husband an unexpected Christmas gift—a cracked skull. She has the whole thing planned perfectly: She'll toss his body down the basement steps, then claim he fell and was killed accidentally, thus assuring that she'll cash in on his sizable insurance policy. Her plan is complicated by only two things. First, her young daughter is just upstairs, anxiously awaiting the arrival of Santa Claus. Second, Santa is on the way. Or rather, a murderous maniac wearing a Santa suit has just escaped from a mental institution.

The wife hears this disquieting news when a bulletin interrupts the soothing Christmas carols on the radio that serve as the sequence's sole musical soundtrack. As luck would have it, this killer Santa heads straight for Joan's house. She runs about frantically locking windows, even as she tries to attend to the cleaning up of the mess that is inevitable when one bludgeons someone on a snow-white carpet—bad planning on her part. Just when it occurs to her that old Santa might be of some use—she can call the cops and claim that *he* killed poor hubby—her young daughter's impatience wins out. She goes to the door and lets Santa in...

When *Tales from the Crypt* was adapted into an

acclaimed and long-running television series on HBO in 1989, a remake of "...And All through the House" was the third episode that aired. Directed by Robert Zemeckis (*Back to the Future*, *Who Framed Roger Rabbit*, *Forrest Gump*), the half-hour treatment starred Mary Ellen Trainor, Zemeckis's wife, as the murderess and Larry Drake (of television's *LA Law*) as the crazed Santa. This

John Carradine in *Silent Night, Bloody Night.*

treatment was substantially more violent and disturbing than the 1972 version–although the grim humor of the original EC story is also in evidence. The main difference between both film versions and the comic book is that the comic story ends as the daughter lets Santa in, allowing the reader to guess what horrors lie in store for Mom. But movie viewers don't like to guess, and in both the feature and the HBO episode, we see what Santa does, in graphic detail.

Another British variation on the murderous Santa theme, *Don't Open 'til Christmas* (1984), came hard on the heels of *Silent Night, Deadly Night*. This one, starring

Caroline Munro, Edmund Purdom (who also directed), and Alan Lake, is about another fellow who has definite issues with Christmas. He goes around murdering department store Santas (rather, Father Christmases) in variously gruesome ways—he burns one, strangles another, dismembers a third, and castrates a fourth. With *Elves* (1988), that makes at least two department store Santas

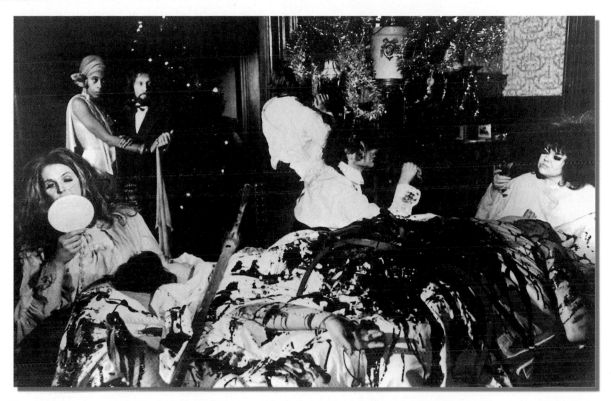

The bloody aftermath of a Christmas party gone wrong in *Silent Night, Bloody Night*.

who have been castrated on film; whether this is the beginning of a trend in evil Christmas movies is anyone's guess.

At least *Don't Open 'til Christmas* didn't have a sequel. *Silent Night, Deadly Night* did. In fact, to date there have been four sequels, which is a fact more frightening than anything in those films.

Actually, for the first hour or so, *Silent Night, Deadly Night Part II* (1987) seems eerily like *Silent Night, Deadly Night Part I*. This one is about Ricky (Eric Freeman), the younger brother of Billy in Part I. As the film begins, a prison psychiatrist interviews Ricky, which gives him, and the filmmakers, a dandy excuse to recount the events of the first movie in great detail. Basically, Ricky has caught the family disease: He likes to punish the "naughty" in brutal and relatively imaginative ways. He repeatedly runs over one man with his own Jeep and jabs an umbrella through another (it opens on the other side). Then he makes a brief stab at being normal by dating luscious Jennifer (Elizabeth Kaitan). To make a good impression on her, he takes her to the movies to see (and I'm not making this up) *Silent Night, Deadly Night*. For good measure, he kills a guy in the theater.

Mr. Sims (Britt Leach, *right*) warns Billy (Robert Brian Wilson) about the perils of drinking at the Christmas party in *Silent Night, Deadly Night*.

Later, Ricky snaps more or less for good and goes on a completely random killing spree; he isn't after the naughty anymore—anyone will do. It isn't until the last act that anyone remembers that the film is set at Christmas time, and Ricky contrives to dress up like Santa for one last brutal murder. He goes after the Mother Superior from the first film (whose street address is 666), and the stage is set for Part III.

The full title of the second sequel is a marquee busting *Silent Night, Deadly Night III: Better Watch Out!* (1989). In many ways, this one is several notches above the previous two. The cast—including Samantha Scully, Eric DaRe, and Laura Herring—is good and even contains a couple of names: Richard Beymer and Robert Culp. Part III was directed by Monte Hellman, one of the most interesting and unusual modern filmmakers and the director of fascinating cult classics like *Two-Lane Blacktop* (1971), *Cockfighter* (1974), and *China 9 Liberty 37* (1978). Hellman's touch is evident in the film's measured pacing and subversive humor. However, it's difficult to know whether his complete disregard for logic and plausibility is just laziness or postmodern satire of the form.

Silent Night, Deadly Night Part III: Better Watch Out! once again introduces us to Ricky, this time played by Bill Moseley. A complete vegetable after the supposedly fatal shootout at the end of the previous film (the shooting was

In *Silent Night, Bloody Night,* the lunatics take over the asylum.

so terrible it changed his face and body type), Ricky lies in a coma, with a clear plastic dome protecting his exposed brain. Luckily for the plot, Ricky is under the care of the strange Dr. Newbury (Beymer), who is trying to establish a telepathic bond between Ricky and Laura (Scully), a blind girl who has volunteered for dream therapy.

Naturally, the connection succeeds terrifically, to the extent that Ricky can "hear" Laura wherever she is. Laura doesn't have quite the same gift, but then if she did, the movie would be much shorter.

Laura, her brother Chris (DaRe), and his new girlfriend (Herring) head up to Grandma's house for Christmas. Ricky escapes the hospital, after waking up and refreshing himself with a couple of bloody murders, then "hears" Laura giving directions. In a hospital gown, barefoot, and

The one and only elf in *Elves*.

with a throbbing brain clearly visible under his dome, Ricky then walks over to the 101 freeway and hitches a ride north.

Ricky's next victim offers the occasion for a little Hellman in-joke. Just before he loses his head, literally, the manager of a remote gas station watches on television Roger Corman's *The Terror* (1960), starring Boris Karloff and a young Jack Nicholson. Hellman, who got his start with Corman, served as second unit director on *The Terror*, and Nicholson later starred in two of Hellman's most acclaimed films: *Ride in the Whirlwind* (1966) and *The Shooting* (1966).

Once the kids get to Grandma's house, they find that Ricky got there first; hence, no more Grandma. At this point, the film turns into the usual "there's-a-maniac-in-the-house movie"—except this one is even more infuriating than most. The characters act with such limitless stupidity that it is impossible to muster up even the most rudimentary sympathy for them. Here are a few examples:

When they arrive, they find that their grandmother isn't there. They spoke with her only minutes before on the phone, and she asked them to pick up something on the way because she didn't feel like going out. Food is boiling away on the stove, and yet they aren't the slightest bit concerned that she isn't there.

Later, Ricky, for reasons of his own, takes their car and crashes it. When they discover that their car has been destroyed, they go walking about in the night shouting, "Granny!"

But the three don't hold a copyright on stupidity. Dr. Newbury and Lt. Connely (Culp), a detective, are speeding their way toward the scene. They learn that they're only fifteen minutes from Granny's house. They hope that they're not too late, tension is mounting—so Connely pulls over to the side of the road to urinate.

Silent Night, Deadly Night III takes place at Christmas, but Christmas is no longer essential to the plot. It would be even less so in the next two entries: *Silent Night, Deadly Night 4: Initiation* (1990), about a woman reporter who gets mixed up with a coven of feminists (again, I'm not making this up), and *Silent Night, Deadly Night 5: The Toy Maker* (1992), about murderous toys.

The one note of interest concerning Part 4 comes from a review by the American Humane Society, which points out that in this movie:

Numerous insects such as roaches and ants are used at various times. In one scene Fima (Maud Adams) commands Kim (Neith Hunter) to eat an insect, but that is never shown on camera. As part of the initiation ritual a mole is sacrificed. For this scene a mole was held by the actress who placed a fake knife made of balsa wood to the side of the mole's throat. The knife was rigged so that stage blood would ooze from the blade. The mole was handled carefully and was never harmed.

American Humane was on the set and we are rating *Initiation* "Acceptable."

They might have been the only organization or person anywhere who thought so.

Christmas carries its own tensions (although sacrificing a mole is done in so few homes these days that it barely deserves mention). There is something awfully cathartic about seeing your worst, most evil thoughts about the holiday made real on the screen in a Christmas horror movie. Granted, most of these movies aren't very good. But in the right mood, they can be at least effective and at most great fun. Always find time at Christmas to watch *The Bishop's Wife* or *Scrooge*. But make a little time for *Black Christmas*, too. Sugar plums dance so much better in your head if occasionally joined by some genuine shivers.

Chapter Six

The Great Christmas Movies

Three Godfathers

ETER B. KYNE'S Western Christmas allegory, *Three Godfathers*, has spawned no less than seven screen incarnations. Originally published as "Broncho Billy and the Baby" in a 1910 edition of *The Saturday Evening Post*, the story evolved first into a 1911 one-reeler film, *The Outlaw and the Child*, starring Broncho Billy Anderson, and

then into a 1913 novel, a morality tale ideal for the movies. Kyne transferred the Nativity story of the Three Wise Men and the birth of Jesus to a late 1800's Western locale, complete with pioneering saints and frontier sinners. Three "good bad men" rob the bank of New Jerusalem and hightail it into the desert. The posse refuses to follow, realizing the outlaws are heading straight into an inescapable desert oven. In the sandy inferno, the three desperados happen upon an abandoned wagon, where a young woman is dying of thirst, a newborn babe nestled in her arms. Before she dies, she ekes a promise from the trio—save her child at all costs.

The three unlikely wet nurses continue their trek across the desert, two of them succumbing to thirst and the elements, leaving one lone gunman to stagger over the burning sands, protecting the baby and honoring the promise made to the mother. On Christmas morning, the survivor makes it back to New Jerusalem, delivering the child to a congregation gathered to celebrate the birth of Christ. By saving the infant, he redeems his outlaw soul before dying on the church floor.

Two subsequent versions of this story, both silent, are regrettably lost films. In 1916, Bluebird released a six-reel version starring Western icon Harry Carey and directed by Edward LeSaint (later a prolific character actor). Three years later, Universal remade the story as *Marked Men* (1919), again with Carey as the lead outlaw but directed this time by twenty-three-year-old Jack Ford, a filmmaker who would become one of the greatest directors in history– John Ford. The young Ford, born Sean Aloysius Feeney, had already directed thirty-one Westerns, most with Carey as the character Cheyenne Harry. According to contemporary reviews, Carey maintained this persona– and character name–for *Marked Men*. Joining him were J. Farrell MacDonald as Placer McGraw and Joe Harris as Tom Gibbons. Location filming took place in the Mojave Desert, with Universal City's Western street doubling for New Jerusalem. Originally titled *The Trail of Shadows*, *Marked Men* was released on December 21, 1919, providing a major Christmas attraction for the burgeoning Universal Pictures. Ford told Peter Bogdanovich in 1964 that he considered *Marked Men* his favorite among his early films.

The next screen incarnation, *Hell's Heroes* (1930), was Universal's first outdoor talking picture. It was directed by another young man destined for greatness, twenty-seven-year-old William Wyler (of *Ben-Hur* and *The Best Years of Our Lives*). Charles Bickford, Raymond Hatton, and Fred Kohler played the three godfathers, from a script by Tom Reed. Wyler took his cameras to the Panamint Valley and the Mojave Desert in a quest for realism, shooting both silent and sound versions.

For years the talkie was considered lost, but it has recently resurfaced courtesy of Turner Entertainment. It's a revelation worthy of rediscovery. Raoul Walsh's *In Old Arizona* and Victor Fleming's *The Virginian*, both from 1929, are often cited as pictures that helped liberate the sound camera from its bulky confines, but seen seventy years later, *Hell's Heroes* emerges as a far more fluid and accomplished film. Wyler keeps the dialogue sparse and the camera moving, maintaining a swiftly paced narrative of just sixty-five minutes. He innovatively uses interior voice-over monologue (when Bickford almost gives up at the poisoned water hole) two years before Rouben Mamoulian's *City Streets*. Using Universal's famous *Broadway* crane (built for Paul Fejos's 1929 film), Wyler also creates a stunning tracking shot of Bickford carrying the baby through a windstorm, the camera soaring upwards to show his solitude.

Fritzi Ridgeway in *Hell's Heroes* (1930).

Hell's Heroes is stark and unsentimental, by far the most unrelenting of extant versions, with desert sequences that compare favorably to Stroheim's *Greed* (1924). Wyler's three godfathers are hard-core outlaws, and there's even the pre-Code suggestion of rape when they find the woman in the wagon. Universal opened the movie in New York on December 27, 1929, and throughout the rest of the country during the first week of January 1930, to great popular and critical success. Darryl Zanuck, head of production at Warner Bros., was so impressed with the filmmaking that he insisted all Warner's staff directors study *Hell's Heroes*.

M-G-M produced the next version, the seldom-seen *Three Godfathers* from 1936. William Wellman (*Wings*, *The Public Enemy*) was originally assigned to direct, but M-G-M switched him to the romantic comedy *Small Town Girl* and brought on Richard Boleslavski (*Rasputin and the Empress*, *Les Miserables*) instead. This time around the outlaws were played by Chester Morris (as Bob Sangster), Lewis Stone (as Doc), and Walter Brennan (as Gus), with their characters considerably softened by producer Joseph L. Mankiewicz (later the director of *All about Eve* and *Cleopatra*). Morris was made a romantic lead and given a love interest in Irene Hervey. Stone was an intellectual bad man, quoting from *Macbeth*, and Brennan, in one of his first important roles, offered comedic relief. Boleslavski remained faithful to Kyne's story, and like his predecessors, Ford and Wyler, shot the desert sequences on location in the Mojave. Filmed from November 27, 1935, through January

Chester Morris in *Three Godfathers* (1936).

Harry Carey Jr., John Wayne, and Pedro Armendariz
in *Three Godfathers* (1948).

4, 1936, and missing a Christmas release, it opened in March to disappointing business.

The best known version of *Three Godfathers* is undoubtedly John Ford's 1948 film, produced by his Argosy Pictures and released through M-G-M. At Harry Carey's funeral in September 1947, Ford told his widow that he would remake their 1919 *Marked Men*. As a gesture to his old friend, Ford dedicated the new picture "To the memory of Harry Carey—bright star of the early Western sky." Ford took the tribute one step further by hiring Harry Carey Jr., nicknamed "Dobie," to play one of the godfathers. Carey Jr. joined reigning box office king John Wayne and Mexican movie star Pedro Armendariz Jr. as the outlaws, with a Ford regular, Ward Bond, playing their pursuer. Laurence Stallings, Frank Nugent, and Robert Nathan (uncredited) wrote the screenplay, with Ford changing the characters' names—Wayne is Robert Marmaduke Sangster Hightower, Armendariz plays Pedro Roca Fuerte, and Carey "the Abilene Kid." The company shot for thirty-two grueling days on location in Death Valley, with another week at the RKO-Pathe Studios in Culver City. The cantankerous Ford was not in good humor on the difficult shoot and unleashed a constant stream of verbal abuse at Armendariz and young Carey, detailed in Carey's memoir, *A Company of Heroes*.

Three Godfathers is one of Ford's minor works and has not sustained a very high critical reputation, mainly because it is as sentimental as Wyler's version is harsh. Ford also lays on the Christian symbolism a bit thick, even for him. The movie's Nativity parable, for example, directed with nuance and grace by Wyler and Boleslavski, is handled in an explicit, heavy-handed manner by Ford. For the first time, the story is even given a happy ending; instead of dying, Wayne's character survives and is sentenced to a year in jail, after which he can come back and be reunited with his godson.

John Wayne in *Three Godfathers* (1948).

Three Godfathers is, however, one of Ford's most visually arresting films, thanks to the exquisite Technicolor cinematography by Winton C. Hoch. Since the movie had no female love interest for Wayne, M-G-M insisted that it be shot in color to give it more box office appeal. In an interview with John Andrew Gallagher in 1978, Hoch considered *Three Godfathers* "a neglected picture, and pretty affecting. I never saw Ford's original silent picture, and just shot this one cold turkey."

Like Carey, Hoch remembered working with Ford and his penchant for testing his coworkers: "He would just love to get you in a spot and hang yourself. We were all ready to work one day and he turned around and asked me, 'What direction you wanna shoot this morning?' The answer's very simple. If you start telling a director which direction to shoot, you better start telling him how to stage his action. I said, 'Any direction you wanna shoot, Jack, is okay with me.' All I had to do was open my face and make a suggestion, I would've been chewed up and spit out in little pieces.

"With the actors it was the same way. He challenged them to give a performance. Once in a while Duke would ask for a change in some lines he had. He just couldn't get the words out in a proper way. He'd say, 'Jack, I just can't say those. Can I change it to so and so?' Jack said, 'Tell it to me again.' Duke spoke it the way he wanted to, the way he felt he could, and Jack would say okay. It meant the same thing but it was just a difference in being comfortable.

"It was a great outfit to work with. There was a great rapport among the cast and crew, but there was very definitely one man who was boss. Ford ran the show and that was it. He rarely bothered me and let me set my own compositions, but we agreed pretty well." For Hoch, his work with Ford ultimately represented "blood, sweat, and hard work."

Three Godfathers was released on December 1, 1948, taking full advantage of the Christmas season. It was only a modest success—for a John Wayne movie. It contained far too little action for his fans. Today it's a television staple during the holidays, a unique Christmas story set in the blistering desert. As is so often the case, television's powers-that-be could not leave well enough alone. In 1974

Christian Bale are outstanding, the picture suffers from some rather anachronistic casting, particularly Susan Sarandon as the girls' mother, spouting nineties feminist platitudes. Critics and audiences were pleased with the updating, and in the year of *Pulp Fiction* and *Forrest Gump*, *Little Women* garnered three Oscar nominations, for Thomas Newman's score, Colleen Atwood's costume design, and for Winona Ryder as Best Actress.

Although Ryder was honored with a nomination, this was perhaps more from a lack of worthy nominees than any greatness in her performance. It was, after all, a terrible year for Hollywood actresses, evidence of the lack of strong roles for women. The other nominees were Jodie Foster in *Nell*, Miranda Richardson for *Tom and Viv*, Susan Sarandon for *The Client*, and Jessica Lange, who won for *Blue Sky*, a film shot *four* years before the awards. Winona Ryder has excelled when cast in contemporary roles like *Heathers* (1989), *Edward Scissorhands* (1990), *Mermaids* (1990), and *Reality Bites* (1994). However, in period pieces (including Coppola's gorgeous vampire opera, *Bram Stoker's Dracula*, but especially in Scorsese's ersatz Merchant-Ivory, sleep-inducing, homage-to-period-props *Age of Innocence* and the misbegotten 1996 *The Crucible*), she simply seems like a twentieth-century visitor stuck in a time warp.

Left to right: Christian Bale, Winona Ryder, Trini Alvarado, and Eric Stoltz star in *Little Women* (1994).

This criticism goes double for Claire Danes, who sealed her incompatibility with period roles with a film-ruining, accent-shifting performance in the otherwise admirable *Les Miserables* (1998). Some actors are just not believable as characters from another century.

With the critical reception heaped upon the 1994 *Little Women*, one has to wonder if nineties reviewers had ever seen the best version ever made–David O. Selznick's 1933 RKO production directed by George Cukor. Selznick was known for his fidelity in adapting classic literature for film (*David Copperfield*, *A Tale of Two Cities*, *Gone with the Wind*), but *Little Women* was his first effort in that arena. In a year of Mae West sex comedies and dozens of gangster pictures, *Little Women* was a refreshing change of pace for

Depression audiences, and even today, the film achieves charming perfection.

Katharine Hepburn had one of her greatest roles as Jo, and indeed, it is disconcerting to watch anyone else in the part. Joan Bennett (pregnant through much of the shoot) portrayed the beautiful but selfish Amy, with Frances Dee as Meg, Jean Parker as Beth, Spring Byington as Marmee, and Paul Lukas as Bhaer, the poor German professor who helps Jo become a writer. Louise Closser Hale started filming the role of Aunt March, but she died during production and was replaced by Edna May Oliver.

Clockwise from left: Margaret O'Brien, Janet Leigh, June Allyson, Elizabeth Taylor, and Mary Astor star in *Little Women* (1949).

Like other great Christmas movies (*It's a Wonderful Life*, *Meet Me in St. Louis*, *A Christmas Story*), family values are front and center in *Little Women*. It has a timeless, heartwarming appeal, full of emotional highs and lows. Cukor conveys an infectious joy as the girls wait to give Christmas presents to Marmee, then subtly shifts the scene into pathos as she thanks them, then suggests they give the presents and their special breakfast to an ailing neighbor and her children.

Hepburn is an utter delight, full of pepper sliding down the bannister, showing Amy how to act terrified, producing her operatic tragedy, "The Witch's Curse," playing the evil Rodrigo in stage mustache and whiskers, defending her father's absence to cantankerous Edna May Oliver, and taking naive stabs at romance and writing. Beth's death scene is also masterfully done, never falling into the cheap sentiment of later versions.

Little Women was beautifully directed and remained Cukor's favorite film. In *On Cukor*, the director told Gavin Lambert about his initial response to the novel: "When I came to read it, I was startled. It's not sentimental or saccharine, but very strong-minded, full of character, and a wonderful picture of New England family life. It's full of that admirable New England sternness, about sacrifice and austerity. And then Kate Hepburn cast something over it. Like Garbo in *Camille*, she was born to play this part. She's tender and funny, fiercely loyal, and plays the fool when she feels like it. There's a purity about her. She really felt it all very deeply. She's a New England girl who understands all that and has her own family feeling."

Though Selznick left RKO for M-G-M before the picture went into production, he was instrumental in convincing the studio bosses not to modernize the story, and he also hired Cukor and cast Hepburn. Cukor paid expert attention to period detail, engaging famed New York interior decorator Hobe Erwin to recreate Alcott's Concord home for the March house set. With a budget of one million Depression-era dollars, the picture was in production from June 28 to September 2, 1933, and was released in New York on November 16, earning RKO close to a million in profits. At Oscar time, the film was nominated for Best Picture and Best Director and won for Sarah Y. Mason and Victor Heerman's screenplay. (Uncredited contributors to the script included Charles Brackett, John Twist, Wanda Tuchock, Jane Murfin, David Hempstead, Al Block, Salisbury Field, G. B. Stern, and Del Andrews.) Hepburn, who won the 1933 Best Actress Oscar for *Morning Glory*, was awarded the Best Actress Prize for *Little Women* at the following year's Cannes Film Festival.

In 1945, Selznick announced a Technicolor remake of *Little Women*, which would star Jennifer Jones, Shirley Temple, Dorothy McGuire, and Diana Lynn. He built sets, had costumes made, and wanted Cukor to direct. Cukor, however, insisted that Hepburn had already played the definitive Jo, and Selznick abandoned the project, selling the sets, costumes, and rights to M-G-M for the disappointing Mervyn LeRoy film. It's just as well Selznick and Cukor did not do another version, since the first time around they made an enduring classic of American cinema and one of the great Christmas movies.

J. A. G.

Miracle on Main Street (1939)

AN UNPRETENTIOUS B movie from 1939, *Miracle on Main Street* is an early independent film produced by Jack Skirball's Arcadia Pictures. Skirball had hit a box-office homer with the sexploitational *The Birth of a Baby* (1938), a self-released sex education movie that shocked and titillated audiences for twenty years to come with its frank discussion of such taboo topics as intercourse, menstruation, and pregnancy. Obviously looking for a change of pace (if not conscience), Skirball financed *Miracle on Main Street*, a Christmas-themed crime picture.

The story involves a sideshow stripper named Maria, who is brutalized by pschotic hubby Dick (Lyle Talbot). On Christmas Eve, she serves as his accomplice when he attacks an undercover cop. Maria and Dick escape, Maria taking sanctuary in a church. She discovers an abandoned baby lying in the Nativity manger and takes the child, posing as a young mother. She comes to adore the child and ends up winning the sympathy and love of Jim, a ranchman (Walter Abel) who helps her get a job as a fashion designer. When he proposes mar-

Lyle Talbot gets tough with Margo in *Miracle on Main Street*.

riage, Maria is about to break down and tell all, but in the best melodramatic tradition, Dick conveniently reappears. He tries to extort money from Jim and, when that fails, tips off the authorities about Maria's past. The climax comes when Dick is shot dead in a robbery, leaving Maria and Jim to live happily ever after.

Miracle on Main Street had a solid cast for a little programmer. Margo starred as the fallen woman, Maria; the former rumba dancer and Broadway star had impressed audiences in Hecht and MacArthur's *Crime without Passion* (1934), William Wellman's *Robin Hood of El Dorado* (1936), and Frank Capra's *Lost Horizon* (1937). Walter Abel, fresh from Wellman's epic *Men with Wings* (1938) and on his way to a distinguished career as a character actor, was the kindly rancher, and Lyle Talbot was typecast as Dick. Jane Darwell, a year before her Oscar-winning performance in John Ford's *The Grapes of Wrath*, played Maria's landlady, with William Collier Sr., an early twentieth-century Broadway pioneer, as a doctor. *Miracle on Main Street* marked Hungarian director Steve Sekely's American debut.

Margo and Walter Abel in *Miracle on Main Street*.

The picture was shot in late April and early May of 1939 on soundstages at Grand National, an upstart company that debuted in 1936. GN was set to release the picture as

Margo in *Miracle on Main Street.*

well, but by the time it had wrapped production, the company was out of business. Harry Cohn's Columbia Pictures stepped in as distributor.

A Spanish-language version was filmed at the same time, a common practice from 1929 to 1931 but relatively rare by 1939. Mexico City's Margo (born Marie Marguerita Guadalupe Teresa Estela Bolado Castilla y O'Donnell) was retained for the lead; Arturo de Cordova (who later enjoyed a brief stint as a mainstream Hollywood star in such films as *Frenchman's Creek*) was cast as her lover; Jose Crespo played Dick; and Carlos Villarias (title star of the legendary 1931 Spanish-language *Dracula*) took the role of the doctor. Twentieth Century-Fox handled the distribution on this version.

The movie seemed to be a good omen for Skirball; he signed with Harry Cohn and Columbia to supervise their Revolutionary War epic, *The Howards of Virginia* (1940), starring Cary Grant, and went on to produce Alfred Hitchcock's *Shadow of a Doubt* (1943) for Universal. Steve Sekely was not as fortunate; his career stayed mired in the B-movie world of *Miracle on Main Street* with credits like *Revenge of the Zombies* (1943) and *Day of the Triffids* (1963).

J. A. G.

Lyle Talbot goes wrong in *Miracle on Main Street.*

Remember the Night (1940)

Remember the Night, written by Preston Sturges and directed by Mitchell Leisen, is a film that's almost impossible to categorize. It begins like a crime story, becomes a screwball comedy, segues into a mood of intense drama, then slowly becomes a warm, touching, and bittersweet story of spiritual rebirth, budding romance, and the

Barbara Stanwyck and Fred MacMurray in *Remember the Night*.

importance of family. The film is set at Christmas time, but that isn't the only reason to consider it a great Christmas movie. *Remember the Night* offers just the right balance of laughter and tears to create a delicate mood of whimsy, nostalgia, and optimism–the perfect Christmas movie ingredients.

As the film begins, Lee Leander (Barbara Stanwyck) has just been arrested for stealing a jewel bracelet. Attorney John Sargeant (Fred MacMurray) is called in to prosecute the case, but because he is anxious to get out of New York to visit his mother (Beulah Bondi) in Indiana for Christmas, John contrives to get the case postponed until after the first of the year. Later, feeling guilty about consigning Lee to jail over the holidays, John posts bond for her. When she tells him that she is from Indiana, too, he offers to drop her off at her mother's house and pick her up on the way back.

After several comic misadventures on the road–including a memorable scene in which Lee tries to hold a cow still while John milks it into a thermos– things turn serious at Lee's mother's. The old woman's stern, unforgiving nature is what drove Lee away from home in the first place—and, by implication, led her to her life of crime. Her mother now treats her with hateful contempt, so John rescues Lee again, this time offering to take her to *his* mother's for Christmas.

It is here that the film ceases to be merely entertaining and becomes truly magical. For the first time in her life, Lee is exposed to a family that treats each other with love, tolerance, and respect. Accepted unconditionally by John's mother, Aunt Emma (Elizabeth Patterson), and hired hand Willie (Sterling Holloway), Lee finds the first moments of peace and contentment in her life.

Beulah Bondi and Fred MacMurray in *Remember the Night*.

The most memorable moments in Christmas films are usually connected with music, and *Remember the Night* is no exception. After supper, the family retires to the living room where John is coaxed into playing and singing a clumsy version of "Swanee River." Lee says that she studied piano for awhile and sits down at the keyboard. Willie, anxious to show off for this beautiful houseguest, says, "I can sing 'The End of a Perfect Day.'" It turns out that he can, beautifully, in a soft tenor voice. Soon, the other members of the family begin to join in the sentimental old song. Lee looks at them, startled by this moment of pure, unpretentious, unquestioning emotion. As with the folk tune "Barbara Allen" in *Scrooge* (1951), "The End of a Perfect Day" seems to evoke everything lovely—and a bit sad—about Christmas, even though the song itself has nothing to do with the season.

The remainder of Lee's week with John's family is taken up by a series of simple, homely activities: baking popovers, exchanging Christmas presents. On New Year's Eve, they attend a barn dance in which everyone is encouraged to dress in old-fashioned clothes. Tightly bound in a corset and wearing Aunt Emma's never-used wedding dress, Lee is a dream of the past—and the point is that she has left everything behind about her own life, and her own future, if only for these few precious days.

By the end of the visit, John and Lee have fallen in love, of course, which presents them with a ticklish problem. He still has to prosecute her when they return to New

York. And she still has to find a way to redeem herself for the mistakes she has made in her life.

The ending of *Remember the Night* is both honest and satisfying, fulfilling the script's romantic demands without pulling a miraculous solution out of the hat. Its bittersweet quality is consistent with everything that has come before—the end of a perfect movie.

Preston Sturges wrote this script in 1939 under the title "Beyond These Tears" (which was later changed by the studio to the inexplicable "The Amazing Marriage"). That screenplay, according to Sturges biographer James Curtis, "was slow and talky and delicate, uncynical; predictable, but not distressingly so. It flowed well and Sturges grew very proud of it."

Sturges wrote, in his long-unpublished memoir, "Writing *Remember the Night*...almost caused me to commit hara-kiri several times, but I postponed it for some later assignment. The trouble was in finding a way to get some pizzazz into the story. When I had Fred MacMurray, as the district attorney, take Barbara Stanwyck, the girl on trial for theft, up to the mountains to reform her, the script died of pernicious anemia. When I had him take her up because his conscience bothered him for having had her trial continued until after the Christmas season, it perished from lack of oxygen. When I had him take her up moved by charitable impulse and the Yuletide spirit, it expired from galloping eunuchery. So I thought of a novelty. The district attorney takes her up to the mountains for the purpose of violating the Mann Act. This has always been a good second act. It is an act enjoyed by all, one that we rarely tire of, and one not above the heads of the audience."

Of course, in the finished picture, the relationship did not have this salacious tinge; whether it was lost in the translation from script to screen is hard to say.

"As it turned out," Sturges wrote, "the picture had quite a lot of schmaltz, a good dose of schmerz and just enough schmutz to make it box office."

Sturges hoped that he would be allowed to direct "Beyond These Tears" himself, but instead the task was assigned to Mitchell Leisen, who had previously directed Sturges's script *Easy Living* (1938), starring Jean Arthur and Ray Milland. (Sturges would make his directorial debut in 1940 with *The Great McGinty*, the first in a remarkable series of outstanding comedies that he would make over the course of the decade.)

As soon as Leisen took over the project, he began pruning Sturges's script; its 130 pages was far too long for a ninety-minute film. One of the scenes deleted immediately had Lee attend church with John's family and become quite moved by the sermon. Other scenes were filmed, then cut: Lee in jail learning that bond has been posted for her; a party at John's mother's where everyone bobs for apples, and a love scene that occurs late in the film. However, as Leisen biographer David Cherichetti has noted, although the director cut the script, he didn't rewrite any of Sturges's lines.

One other change occurred during production. Actress Marjorie Main, best known for her appearances with Percy Kilbride in the *Ma and Pa Kettle* series, was cast to play Lee Leander's cruel, bitter mother. Eleanor Broder, Leisen's personal secretary, told Cherichetti, "[Main] played it just like a crazy woman. She went into the scene and she lost all control. She threw herself down on a bench and it just wasn't real. After one take, I can remember going up and asking her if she needed some smelling salts." Main was quickly replaced by Georgia Caine, who played the part with a cold sense of hatred–perfect for the role.

Although *Remember the Night* is leisurely paced, its production blazed along like a house afire. Scheduled for forty-two shooting days, Leisen and company brought the film in at only thirty-four days, saving Paramount over $50,000. According to Leisen, all the credit for this speed went to Stanwyck: "Barbara Stanwyck was the greatest. She never blew one line through the whole picture. She set that kind of pace and everybody worked harder, trying to outdo her."

"Stanwyck's performance is one of her finest," wrote Stanwyck biographer Ella Smith. "Lee Leander is a mixture of wit, intelligence and sensitivity–which Stanwyck puts across with the same."

Remember the Night also benefits from the fine, subtle performance by Fred MacMurray. Best known today for his rather one-dimensional role in television's *My Three Sons* and for a few goofy Disney comedies in the fifties and sixties, MacMurray is in serious danger of being under-rated. In fact, he was a remarkably versatile performer who could play a tough-talking thug in one picture, a sensitive romantic type in another, a macho adventurer in a third, and a clumsy goofball in a fourth. His role as John Sargeant in *Remember the Night* calls on most of these skills: He begins as a decent, if somewhat cynical, district attorney, moves into the raucous physical comedy of the second act, and finally becomes a truly appealing romantic lead. Barbara Stanwyck is one of the greatest actresses ever to work in the movies; films like *Remember the Night* prove that Fred MacMurray was just as skilled.

Remember the Night has somehow never garnered the reputation of *Miracle on 34th Street*, *It's a Wonderful Life*, *The Bishop's Wife*, or other recognized Christmas classics. But in its tender sentimentality, its bursts of riotous humor, its dark moments of drama, and its clear-eyed ideas about love, redemption, and the comfort of family, it is the equal of any of them; *Remember the Night* is truly a great Christmas movie.

Christmas in July (1940) and *The Miracle of Morgan's Creek* (1944)

PRESTON STURGES'S *Christmas in July* is not one of his best-remembered pictures, but it is a typically clever and refreshing meditation on the consequences of easy money, set against the backdrop of corporate America and with a healthy dose of social satire.

During the thirties, Sturges had written for such directors as Wyler, Whale, Leisen, and Mamoulian. Most notably, he penned the screenplay for William K. Howard's *The Power and the Glory* (1933), which made use of a complex flashback structure that anticipated Welles's *Citizen Kane* by eight years. In late 1939, Paramount finally allowed Sturges to direct his own script on a shoestring budget, and the result was the political comedy *The Great McGinty*. On the basis of that film's early footage, Paramount gave Sturges the green light for a second picture. Their faith was not misplaced; *McGinty* was a

Ellen Drew and Dick Powell in *Christmas in July*.

financial success and won Sturges an Oscar for Best Screenplay.

For his sophomore film, Sturges dusted off an unproduced three-act play he had written in 1931 entitled *A Cup of Coffee*. He adapted the play for Universal in 1935, but when the studio was sold later that year, the project was shelved. Sturges convinced Paramount to buy back the rights, for which they paid Universal $6,000. Under the title *The New Yorkers*, production began on June 1, 1940, and wrapped on June 29.

The story was as follows: On New York's East Side, Jimmy MacDonald (Dick Powell) dreams of prosperity so

Ellen Drew and Dick Powell in *Christmas in July*.

that he can marry girlfriend Betty Casey (Ellen Drew). While working as a coffee company clerk at Baxter's, Jimmy enters a slogan contest sponsored by the rival, Maxford Coffee Company. Three mischievous friends send him a phony telegram proclaiming that he has won the first prize of $25,000 for his slogan, "If you can't sleep at night, it's not the coffee, it's the bunk." Jimmy wins a promotion at Baxter's and, through a mixup, actually collects the prize money from Maxford. Euphoric, Jimmy buys Betty an engagement ring and creates a "Christmas in July" for their families and neighborhood friends, arriving home with dozens of presents for one and all, including a doll for a little crippled girl and a davenport sofa for his mother. Maxford realizes their mistake but, as a gesture of goodwill, allows everyone to keep their presents. Betty convinces Jimmy's boss to give him a chance, and in a fairy tale ending, the real winner of the slogan contest is announced—Jimmy MacDonald!

Like all of Sturges's films, much of the fun is provided by a supporting cast of wonderful character actors, including William Demaraest as a contest judge, Raymond Walburn as Maxford, and Franklin Pangborn as the radio announcer. Sturges himself makes a cameo appearance as a man at a shoeshine stand. Retitled *Christmas in July* for a late October release, the movie proved popular with audiences and critics alike. Sturges's script was adapted for *Lux Radio Theatre* in 1944, starring Dick Powell and Linda Darnell. Ten years later it was remade for television's *Lux Video Theatre*, with Nancy Gates, Alex Nicol, and Raymond Walburn, reprising his film role.

Although Sturges was by no means Hollywood's first writer-director, his string of Paramount hits from 1940 to 1944 (including *The Lady Eve*, *Sullivan's Travels*, *The Palm Beach Story*, and *Hail the Conquering Hero*) did pave the way for such giants as Billy Wilder, Walter Huston, and Orson Welles. Sturges proved he was capable of calling the shots of production, making the adjustment from writer's cubicle to director's chair with ease. Enjoying a renewed level of appreciation today, his films showcase a creative control that make him an auteur in every sense of that misused word.

J. A. G.

The same year *Christmas in July* was released, Sturges wrote another classic Christmas movie, *Remember the Night*, which is discussed elsewhere in this book. A few years later, he made another film with Christmas overtones. *The Miracle of Morgan's Creek* (1944) is a brilliant comedy starring Betty Hutton as a patriotic young woman, Trudie Kockenlocker, who attends a series of parties one night and is impregnated by a mysterious soldier whose name she can't remember. (She does, however, remember marrying him; this is still, after all, Hollywood under the Production Code.) Her faithful boyfriend (Eddie Bracken) sticks by her, but her shame turns into triumph when she gives birth on Christmas morning to sextuplets—and puts Morgan's Creek on the map by proclamation of Governor McGinty (Brian Donlevy reprising his role from *The Great McGinty*).

The slightly blasphemous notion of Trudie's "virgin birth" kept *The Miracle of Morgan's Creek* out of release until 1944—well over a year after it was completed. But once it finally came out, audiences loved it. So did critics. James Agee marvelled in *The Nation* that "the Hays Office has either been hypnotized into a liberality for which it should be thanked, or it has been raped in its sleep." *The Miracle of Morgan's Creek* was the biggest money-maker of the year and lives on both as a classic frantic comedy and a very peculiar—but great—Christmas movie.

F. T.

Holiday Inn (1942) and *White Christmas* (1954)

IRVING BERLIN is possibly America's greatest song-writer. He is certainly among the most prolific, honored, successful, and influential composers ever. He wrote over 1,500 songs, an impressive number of which have become enduring American classics, and he was even awarded the Congressional Gold Medal for "God Bless America." Like many songwriters of his era, Berlin wrote song scores for many, many films and shows. By the mid-thirties, he was such an institution that entire movies could be built around popular songs he had already written. Twentieth Century-Fox's *Alexander's Ragtime Band* (1938), for example, used no fewer than twenty-three Berlin compositions, a number of which were already beloved classics, including "Blue Skies," "Easter Parade," and the title song.

Bing Crosby and Fred Astaire in *Holiday Inn*.

In 1942 Paramount decided to create another movie for the Berlin catalog. In this case, Berlin himself came up with the story idea: Since he had already written numerous songs about holidays, why not make a *movie* about holidays?

Holiday Inn is about a song and dance team (Bing Crosby and Fred Astaire) who split up when Crosby wants to take it easy up at his country inn. So that he doesn't lose touch with show biz altogether, he decides to turn the inn into a very special kind of nightclub—it will only open eight nights out of the year on holidays.

A sparkling romantic comedy-musical, *Holiday Inn* has achieved classic status because of several incredible

Astaire dance numbers–including a Fourth of July piece in which he dances with lit firecrackers–and its appealing catalog of songs, which include "Easter Parade," "Happy Holidays," "Song of Freedom," and "Let's Start the New

Holiday Inn starring Bing Crosby and Fred Astaire with (*left to right*) Virginia Dale, Walter Abel, and Marjorie Reynolds.

Bing Crosby and Marjorie Reynolds in *Holiday Inn*.

Year Right." But the song that really put *Holiday Inn* on the map was one that Berlin wrote specifically for the film–"White Christmas."

Crosby introduced the song in a duet with co-star Marjorie Reynolds (whose singing voice was dubbed by Martha Mears), and the shock waves continue to this day, well over half a century later. To date, "White Christmas" has sold nearly 40 million copies–the best-selling movie song ever written. It won the Academy Award that year for Best Song; despite numerous nominations, this was Berlin's only Oscar.

"White Christmas" quickly became Crosby's theme song, and he would perform it for the rest of his life. When he and Astaire teamed up again for another Berlin songfest–this time in Technicolor–called *Blue Skies* (1946), Crosby gave "White Christmas" its second cinematic performance.

Its third almost took place in yet another Crosby-Astaire vehicle. But Fred Astaire hated the script of *White*

Christmas (1954) and bowed out. He was replaced by Donald O'Connor, who soon became ill and had to quit the show, too. Directing screenwriters Melvin Frank and Norman Panama had just completed *Knock on Wood* with Danny Kaye, and the head of Paramount asked them to rewrite the script for his talents. They did. Panama said later, "We got practically nothing for it, and [*White Christmas*] plays every Christmas."

Singer Rosemary Clooney was cast as Crosby's love interest and singer-dancer Vera-Ellen signed on as Clooney's sister and Kaye's romantic partner. The director was the legendary Michael Curtiz, the man behind *The Sea Hawk*, *Casablanca*, *Yankee Doodle Dandy*, and scores of other classic films. "Fascinating man," Clooney says. "He was always kind of blustery, but never that way with Bing. Bing set the tone of the picture; he was very easygoing, very professional." Curtiz, a Hungarian, was famous for mangling the English language. "I was climbing out the window in one scene," Clooney recalls, "and he said he wanted me 'a little off from balance.' So you have to kind of figure out what he's talking about. 'Okay, Mike...'"

Danny Kaye and Bing Crosby cut a rug in *White Christmas*.

White Christmas earned a little slice of cinema history by being the first film shot in the new wide-screen format VistaVision. By running the film horizontally through the camera instead of vertically, VistaVision offered a far larger image on the negative than was possible with normal 35 mm film. Using this superior negative, Paramount could offer theaters a VistaVision film in any format they desired: "flat" (the old style, a nearly square picture); 1.85 to 1, the normal wide-screen format; or an anamorphic print similar to the format that Twentieth Century-Fox was using, CinemaScope.

Clooney admits that she wasn't overly conscious of VistaVision except that, for a while, it doubled everyone's work. The studio had decided to hedge its bets by filming *White Christmas* both in VistaVision and in standard 35 mm. "We would get one take with the regular camera and one in VistaVision," she remembers. "But that didn't last very long. Bing *hated* that, and it was decided to just do VistaVision. That was that! Bing wouldn't put up with it."

Danny Kaye was a brilliant performer who was spectacularly talented at comedy, singing, dancing–everything. Clooney remembers that he and Bing got along great both on and off the screen. "Danny brought out the sense of the ridiculous in Bing," she says. "There was one take when Bing just broke up while they were [lip-synching] 'Sisters' to our voices, when Danny hit Bing in the stomach with the fan. Bing just started to laugh. They did another take and printed both of them. But they used the one where Bing broke up."

White Christmas offered viewers a spectacular introduction to VistaVision, and audiences everywhere loved the film. Many of the critics didn't respond so well: "It's not a great picture any way you look at it," wrote columnist W. R. Wilkerson in *The Hollywood Reporter* (January 26, 1955), "but, brother, it's doing great business."

"Its box office success is a foregone conclusion," agreed the *Los Angeles Times*'s Philip K. Scheuer, "but the inescapable final judgment of the reviewer is that it delivers less than it promises."

Where are those critics now?

Today *White Christmas* is just as vibrant, just as enjoyable as it was to those enthusiastic original audiences. The brilliant color, VistaVision cinematography, and stereo sound have been faithfully reproduced on laser disc and, to a lesser extent, on videocassette. Many people don't consider Christmas adequately celebrated until *White Christmas* has been viewed at least once.

Rosemary Clooney suggests that the film remains so popular because of the "combination of Berlin's music and Bing Crosby and Christmas. Put those three things together, you can't resist 'em."

True enough. Especially when you add the stellar contributions of Danny Kaye, Vera-Ellen, and Clooney herself. *White Christmas* may not be the greatest musical in history, but it is warm, entertaining, funny, romantic, and filled with some of the greatest songs ever to come out of Hollywood. It's the perfect memory of Christmases past and a continuing joy for Christmases yet to come.

Meet Me in St. Louis (1944)

VINCENTE MINNELLI'S lavish slice of turn-of-the-century Americana includes one of the movies' most famous Yuletide moments–Judy Garland singing "Have Yourself a Merry Little Christmas" to kid sister Margaret O'Brien. *Meet Me in St. Louis* is a richly Technicolored, nearly perfect film musical, one of the best from producer Arthur Freed's legendary unit at M-G-M. Like *Little Women*, it chronicles a year in the life of a family, in this case, the Smiths of 5135 Kensington Avenue, St. Louis, Missouri, whose lives in an affluent suburb of Victorian charm are chronicled from the summer of 1903 through the spring of 1904 and the opening of the St. Louis World's Fair.

Leon Ames plays Alonzo Smith, "Father,"a lawyer with a healthy respect for routine and the status quo. Mary Astor, as his wife, is the Perfect Movie Mother; oldest daughter Rose (Lucille Bremer) is expecting a proposal of marriage any day; Esther (Judy Garland) falls in love with John Truett (Tom Drake), The Boy Next Door; and the youngest, Tootie (Margaret O'Brien), just loves St. Louis. ("Wasn't I lucky to be born in my favorite city?" she asks early in the film.) Brother Lon Jr. (Henry Daniels Jr. in a role vacated by Van Johnson) is anxious to start college, while Grandpa (Harry Davenport) and Katie the maid (Marjorie Main) provide comic relief. The whole family has an unabashed love affair with the Midwestern metropolis, but at Christmas, Father decides to move the whole family to New York because of business. Everyone is plunged into depression, climaxed by Tootie's destruction of the snowmen she's built on the front lawn. Father realizes his family's happiness is more important than money and decides to stay in St. Louis, "the best city in America." The deliriously happy ending brings the Smiths to the glittery opening of the World's Fair.

The story for *Meet Me in St. Louis* was adapted from Sally Benson's "Kensington Stories," which had appeared in *The New Yorker* magazine from 1941 to 1942, before M-G-M acquired the rights for the Freed unit. With its nostalgic celebration of family values, along with a heaping helping of Mom

June Lockhart, Henry H. Daniels Jr., Harry Davenport, and Judy Garland in *Meet Me in St. Louis*.

Margaret O'Brien lets Judy Garland in on a little secret in *Meet Me in St. Louis.*

and Apple Pie, the material was custom-made for M-G-M chieftain Louis B. Mayer. In typical Metro fashion, a battalion of writers worked on the script, including author Benson, Sarah Y. Mason and Victor Heerman (scripters of the 1933 *Little Women*), Doris Gilbert, and William Ludwig, along with the credited writers, Irving Brecher and Fred Finkelhoffe.

Arthur Freed guided the project with a knowing hand, commissioning Hugh Martin and Ralph Blane to write "Have Yourself a Merry Little Christmas," "The Trolley Song," "The Boy Next Door," and "Under the Bamboo Tree." (The traditional tune "Meet Me in St. Louis" had been written by Andrew Sterling and Kerry Mills in 1903.) George Cukor was set to direct; but when he left to join the signal corps, Vincente Minnelli was given the assignment, only his third feature. With the support of Freed and Mayer, Minnelli steeped the picture in period detail,

Tom Drake, Margaret O'Brien, and Judy Garland in *Meet Me in St. Louis.*

with carefully designed color schemes for each of the four seasons.

At first Kensington Avenue was going to be recreated on the Carvel Street set of the *Andy Hardy* series, but when the studio expanded the production to become one of the year's key releases, they built a whole new street of Victorian houses and manicured lawns (the set was reused

A Smith family dinner often ends in tears in *Meet Me in St. Louis. Left to right*: Joan Carroll, Harry Davenport, Mary Astor, Lucille Bremer, Leon Ames, and Judy Garland.

for dozens of M-G-M films). Production began on November 11, 1943, and was plagued by cast illness (Astor's sinusitis, O'Brien's hay fever, Joan Carroll's emergency appendectomy) and especially by the working habits of Garland. June Lockhart had an early role as a neighbor girl and remembers the shoot as "tedious. We would be in makeup at six AM, but Judy wouldn't come in until noon. Then we'd all go to lunch, come back, and be dismissed. This went on day after day after day. But once she started working, oh, it was heaven. Vincente and Judy seemed terribly professional on the set, but I was oblivious to the fact they were falling in love."

Minnelli recalled, "You could tell Judy twenty different things while she was with the hairdresser or being made up, but you wouldn't know you were getting through to her. It was like talking to a blank wall. But by God, everything was there when the cameras rolled, everything you asked for, and she did it beautifully." Minnelli and Garland married after their next picture together, *The Clock*, in 1945.

Meet Me in St. Louis finally finished shooting on April 7, 1944, $170,000 over its $1.5 million budget. It became a huge hit with wartime audiences, and at Oscar time, it received nominations for screenplay, George Folsey's color cinematography, Best Scoring of a Musical Picture, and Best Song ("The Trolley Song"), with Special Academy Award going to Margaret O'Brien as Outstanding Child Actress of 1944.

"Christmas is something that brings people together," O'Brien comments today. "And *Meet Me in St. Louis* showed how the family came together; they had everything right there at home instead of looking for it somewhere else. The movie is a Christmas tradition. I think to make lasting Christmas movies you have to have warmth. You have to have family and a little comedy and clever writing." *Meet Me in St. Louis* has them all, plus, as O'Brien says, "all those wonderful songs."

J.A.G.

Margaret O'Brien Remembers

✳ ✳ ✳

I have a lot of memories about *Meet Me in St. Louis*, because I almost didn't do *Meet Me in St. Louis*. I was working for M-G-M and had done several pictures, *Journey For Margaret* (1942), *Lost Angel* (1944), and I was making very little money at the time and my mother thought, "You know, I don't know how long my child [can] go on being an actress, so I'm going to tell Mr. Mayer [president of Metro-Goldwyn-Mayer] we want such and such." And of course Mr. Mayer threw a fit at the time when she went into the office, and she said, "That's all right. I don't want my child to work that hard." My mother was a bit of a gypsy, a Spanish gypsy, so we took off and went to Spain and New York.

In those days they had something very interesting at the studio. They had what they called lookalikes. And they had a little girl who looked similar to me, and they put her under contract. They would use these lookalikes if the star got a little bit temperamental or wanted more money or something like that. When the studio couldn't find us, because my mother had taken us to New York, they were panicking. They called this little girl and her family and said that she had *Meet Me in St. Louis* and she was going to play the part of Tootie, never really thinking she was going to play it. This was just sort of a ploy until we got back—and they could do the costumes and she could stand in for the fitting of the costumes and so forth. Finally, they tracked us down in New York and told my mother that they would do everything she asked. And we came back to do *Meet Me in St. Louis*—I loved the script and I really wanted to do it so badly. The only very sad thing was they had to tell this little girl's family that she was not going to be playing the part of Tootie in *Meet Me in St. Louis*. Her father was a lighting technician on the set, and he tried to drop a lamp on me during the shooting of *Meet Me in St. Louis* because they were so distraught over this. But anyway, I did the part and I loved doing that film.

I loved working with Judy Garland because that was a very, very happy time for her. She had just married Vincente Minnelli [actually, Minnelli and Garland would marry in 1945, after their next film together, *The Clock*], and he was a wonderful director to work with. He loved antiques, so he was a master at creating that particular era, that Victorian era. He was such a stickler for detail, and he did all of the antiques him-

Margaret O'Brien starred in several Christmas movies, including *Tenth Avenue Angel* and 1949's remake of *Little Women*.

self. He went and hunted for them. Every doorknob in the house was an antique doorknob, which I wish I had today. Every ornament on the tree. I'd just stare at that tree in awe! But I just admired him so much for doing all that. And he really created the whole atmosphere and ambience of that film. Judy was wonderful. I didn't have any sisters so she was the older sister I would have loved to have had. And I got to play a little bit of a brat in that film. Normally I was a little quiet as a child and very serene and wasn't really a brat at all. So this was fun. I got to do all the things I

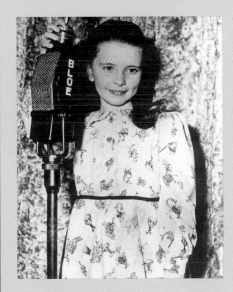

Margaret O'Brien in a photo from her private collection.

wasn't allowed to do at home. I really, really did enjoy that. And of course it being a wonderful Christmas film, too. I loved Christmas and I didn't see a lot of snow out here in California. They built snowmen on the set with dry ice and I loved all my snowmen, just like the little girl in the film.

Tootie had a real morbid streak. She loved to bury her dolls in the cemeteries; maybe that's where I got it from. I had a big doll collection, and when I was making *Bad Bascomb* (1946), up in Wyoming, I loved being with the Indians. I spent a lot of time with the Apache tribe up in Wyoming, so when I got home, I scalped all my dolls. So it was a little bit like Tootie–except she buried hers.

"Have Yourself a Merry Little Christmas"–that was a very dramatic scene because the whole family was supposed to be leaving St. Louis and none of us wanted to leave, and I especially did not want to leave my snowmen and go to another place for Christmas. So Judy was trying to make me feel better and she was going to sing this song to me. But when she received the lyrics of the song, "Have Yourself a Merry Little Christmas," it was not at all what she wanted. It was sort of like, this will be our last Christmas, we can't have a Merry Little Christmas because it's our last, and now we'll have to think of things in the past. And she said, "Oh, I can't sing this to little Margaret O'Brien, especially when she's supposed to be crying over losing her snowmen and not being able to take them to this other city." So she had the people rewrite the song. Of course they were very grateful to her later because that's what made it such a great hit. And she lightened it up and made it so that she was trying to make me happy instead of being doomy and gloomy, too. And of course we have that every year now, "Have Yourself a Merry Little Christmas." And every Christmas it brings back memories to me; that was one of my favorite scenes.

Well, there's been so many stories about how they got me to cry for that scene in *Meet Me in St. Louis*. And there's been rumors–I think even Vincente Minnelli wrote in his book that they had told me that my dog had died. Well, my mother wouldn't have allowed that. I know they did it in the past to Jackie Cooper, and he's still traumatized by that today. So my mother would never have allowed that. But how she got me to cry was that June Allyson, who had played my sister in several films, was another big crier in her pictures. So we were known as the Town Criers of M-G-M and we were sort of in competition–who could cry bigger tears. So all my mother would have to do, if I had a hard time crying–which I did at the beginning of that scene–she came up to me and said, "Well, maybe I'll have the makeup man put false tears" because sometimes they would come and squirt false tears if an actor or actress couldn't cry. And I thought, "Oh no. That's terrible. They'll say I can't cry real tears." Mother said, "No, they'll just squirt the water on–but I'm sure that June would never do that. Her tears are always real." And that worked like a charm! I burst into tears whenever that makeup man came anywhere near me! And that's how I cried those big tears in that scene.

As a child, when I was doing films, I took it very seriously. I took it as a job that I was doing and I wanted to do the best job I could. And I wanted to really do a good scene. So I just sort of got in the mood. I thought of June again and her tears and came down and smashed these snowmen, which I would never do to my own snowmen, but it was something that I knew that Tootie would do. So I sort of got in the mood for that and always wanted to do the best I could do for the studio. And felt that I was there to do a job and of course once the scene was over I had a wonderful capacity, and I still have that today, thank goodness, to forget all about it. Two minutes later I was out eating a hot dog or playing with the little girl who was my stand-in, and we were skipping rope or something like that. So I could get over it very quickly.

Meet Me in St. Louis was a successful film. I don't think that when we were making it that everybody thought it was going to be the classic it became, but right from the start, it was a very happy set. We all got along. The family was really like a family and that was what made the picture work. Judy and I got along very well, and Lucille Bremer, who was the older sister, was wonderful to work with. Harry Davenport, the gentleman that played my grandfather, Marjorie Main, Joan Carroll, who was the middle sister, Tom Drake, who was the boy next door. Everybody got along and everybody enjoyed each other and that's what went to make the warmth in this family that you really had to portray in this film. It came across right away in the rushes, and the studio was excited about the film at the time.

Now, *Meet Me in St. Louis* is really a Christmas tradition. Before we had tape, they had put it in a time capsule to be opened in the year 2000-something. Of course when tape came, it was preserved to be on that. But it was so authentic, the houses and the street–that's why the *Meet Me in St. Louis* street was really a tourist attraction for many years at the studio,

Margaret O'Brien and Judy Garland perform a cakewalk in *Meet Me in St. Louis*.

because of the quality of the Victorian homes that were built for that movie. It really shows a family of the early 1900s, and it's something that we today, or future generations, can look back and see what that time was like and see it authentically.

And of course I love Christmas myself. It's always been my favorite time of the year. And as a child, of course, doing *Meet Me in St. Louis*, I had two of my favorite holidays, because one of my favorites was Halloween, and I had a big Halloween scene in *Meet Me in St. Louis*, and then I had Christmas too. So that's one of the reasons I loved doing that movie.

Tenth Avenue Angel (1948)

Tenth Avenue Angel was a movie I made after *Meet Me in St. Louis*. And of course I had another Christmas theme in that movie where I was a rather poor little girl and my mother [Phyllis Baxter] had struggled all of her life. Then she became ill, and I had always been religious—my mother had taught me to be very religious. And I had a cow, like a little ceramic cow, and she said the cow was religious and went back to the Nativity days. Then I lost faith after my mother became ill, and there was a scene where George Murphy and Angela Lansbury, who were also friends of my mother's, told me to keep praying and pray for my mother and she would be better. As I was praying, there was a cow in a barn and the cow knelt and that was a symbol to me that my mother would be all right and that I kept my faith. And that was more or less what that film was all about.

Angela Lansbury was wonderful to work with. Of course, in recent years I worked with her on her television show [*Murder, She Wrote*] and that was so much fun to be reunited in later years. We were also reunited with some other wonderful actresses, Jane Withers, Marie Windsor. We had a lot of fun. It was a great reunion.

I think that Christmas is something that brings people together. *Meet Me in St. Louis* showed how the family came together and the father realized money wasn't that important. His job in the other city was going to pay a lot more money, and the house would be bigger and grander. But he realized that it was more important to just stay in their own hometown that they loved so much, that they had everything right there instead of

looking for it somewhere else, and that the family was the most important, to keep his family happy. And that sort of was the theme of that
Christmas. *Tenth Avenue Angel* showed that if you keep the faith, things
will be better–don't lose faith. Its theme was more appropriate to the religious side of Christmas. So I've done Christmas movies with different
views.

Little Women (1949)

I loved doing *Little Women* because I loved the book so much. And of
course, it's Christmas again, where all the girls would get together and
make their little Christmas ornaments because we didn't have a lot of
money in *Little Women*. There was a scene where our mother [Mary Astor,
also the mother in *Meet Me in St. Louis*] had brought all the girls these
wonderful popovers for Christmas breakfast. And we were all eating them
and having wonderful time. I played Beth, the really caring sister, and
there was a poor family that lived down the hill that my mother would go
see and take care of. And I started to think while we were eating these bis-
cuits that the family didn't have any, and, you know, we were eating too
many and we should save some and bring some to this family. At first Amy
[Elizabeth Taylor], who was the more selfish sister, didn't want to give up
her popovers, but then after a while, all of the girls realized that we just
had to bring some to this family. So that sort of brought all the sisters
together and they gave up something of theirs for Christmas to make
somebody else happy. That's another very nice Christmas theme, isn't it–
the spirit of giving.

I think that people do come together at Christmas time and sometimes
we forget about that theme during the year. But thank goodness that at
least once a year at Christmas it kind of renews our thoughts about things
that we really should be doing. Christmas makes people think about their
lives and about things they could do that are better for the next year. It's a
wonderful time of year.

Christmas Holiday (1944)

IT IS AMUSING to imagine a moviegoer of 1944 thumbing through the newspaper ads, trying to decide which film to go out and see. His eyes light on *Christmas Holiday*. Even though it's the middle of June, that sounds like a pleasant picture. Who does it star? Deanna Durbin and Gene Kelly. Ah, a musical. Well, that *would* be nice.

But soon it becomes evident that all is not right with this film. Even though Deanna sings a song or two, this is no musical. In fact, *Christmas Holiday* is a darkly dramatic film noir, a story of murder, robbery, and betrayal.

Based on the novel by Somerset Maugham, *Christmas Holiday* is about Abigail Martin (Durbin), a young woman recently moved to New Orleans who meets a charming ne'er-do-well, Robert Manette (Kelly), and falls in love with him. After gaining the approval of his rather intense mother (Gale Sondergaard), they marry—and the trouble begins. He is a gambler and petty thief and soon murders a bookie. He is sentenced to prison for the crime, and Abigail changes her name to Jackie Lamont and takes a job as singer and "hostess" in a local roadhouse.

We learn all this in flashback on a stormy Christmas Eve. Charles Mason (Dean Harens), an army lieutenant recently jilted by his fiancee, is delayed in New Orleans and meets Abigail/Jackie at the roadhouse ("Maison Lafitte"). She begs him to take her to midnight mass, and there breaks down in sobs as the choir sings "Adeste Fideles." Charles takes her to a diner where she tells him the sad story of her life with Manette. Of course, as it turns out, the story really isn't over yet.

Christmas Holiday was seen as a drastic departure for Durbin. She had been Universal's biggest star since 1936 and *Three Smart Girls*; all of her films were charming comedies with plenty of music, each of them emphasizing her youth and freshness. Now, at twenty-two she was taking on her first truly adult role in her first serious film. Indeed, as directed by master of the film noir Robert Siodmak, *Christmas Holiday* was more than serious—it was downright bleak.

It was, however, not nearly as bleak as it might have been. Hollywood under the Production Code could not honestly adapt Maugham's novel; there were too many taboos, according to the censors. The relationship of the

Deanna Durbin and Gene Kelly in *Christmas Holiday*.

mother and son in the book had clear overtones of incest. In the film, Durbin's character says that they had a "pathological" relationship but lets it go at that. Also, Abigail in the book becomes a prostitute after Robert is sent to prison. To have Deanna Durbin play a prostitute would have been more of a stretch than even the most demanding critics would have wanted. Instead, she's a singer and hostess at Maison Lafitte. Abigail/Jackie is ordered to be nice to the clients, but in the film's terms that means only that she sits and makes small talk while they buy drinks. One critic (*Los Angeles Times*, July 4, 1944) "trusts that Somerset Maugham has a sense of humor. He is going to need it when he sees what Universal has done with his novel, the changes made to give his prostitute great strength of character and purification so that Deanna Durbin won't be cheapened by the character she portrays."

The role of the petty crook-turned-murderer was not a stretch for Gene Kelly. Still a relative newcomer—he had made his debut in 1942 with Judy Garland in *For Me and My Gal*—Kelly had divided his roles between musicals like *DuBarry Was a Lady* (1943) and dramatic films such as *Pilot No. 5* (1943) and *The Cross of Lorraine* (1943). As often as not, these early characters were unsympathetic, arrogant, and hotheaded. In fact, Edwin Schallert in the *Los Angeles Times* (June 30, 1944) wrote, "Kelly gets mean duty to do once again, even though he is allowed to present an ingratiating personality. He's a merciless avenger of supposed wrongs to himself."

Film historian Jeanine Basinger says that *Christmas Holiday* "laid an egg at the box office because people's expectations were not met. It's a totally misleading title. And I notice that sometimes when I'm looking at research material, people identify that movie as a musical, because of its stars."

But to Basinger, *Christmas Holiday* created a true Christmas memory. Her mother, much like the fictional moviegoer above, sent young Jeanine off to the movies, confident that she would be seeing a nice Deanna Durbin musical. "That was one of my mother's great mistakes in life," Basinger says, "letting me sneak off to that movie. It was actually a film noir, a tragic movie full of murder and death and degradation. I had a great Christmas experience at that movie, by the way. I was happy to see it."

Christmas in Color

"Fred's a lucky young devil... I wish you both great happiness!"

Charles Dickens'
A CHRISTMAS CAROL
A Metro-Goldwyn-Mayer Picture

M·G·M's MEET ME IN ST. LOUIS
GLORIOUS LOVE STORY WITH MUSIC
Starring JUDY Garland
with MARGARET O'BRIEN
MARY ASTOR LUCILLE BREMER
TOM DRAKE MARJORIE MAIN
SCREEN PLAY BY IRVING BRECHER AND FRED F. FINKLEHOFFE
BASED ON THE BOOK BY SALLY BENSON
A METRO-GOLDWYN-MAYER PICTURE
DIRECTED BY VINCENTE MINNELLI
PRODUCED BY ARTHUR FREED
Photographed in TECHNICOLOR
Copyright 1944 Loew's Incorporated
Country of Origin U. S. A.
Property of National Screen Service Corp. Licensed for display only in connection with the exhibition of this picture at your theatre. Must be returned immediately thereafter.
Tooker Litho Co. N.Y.

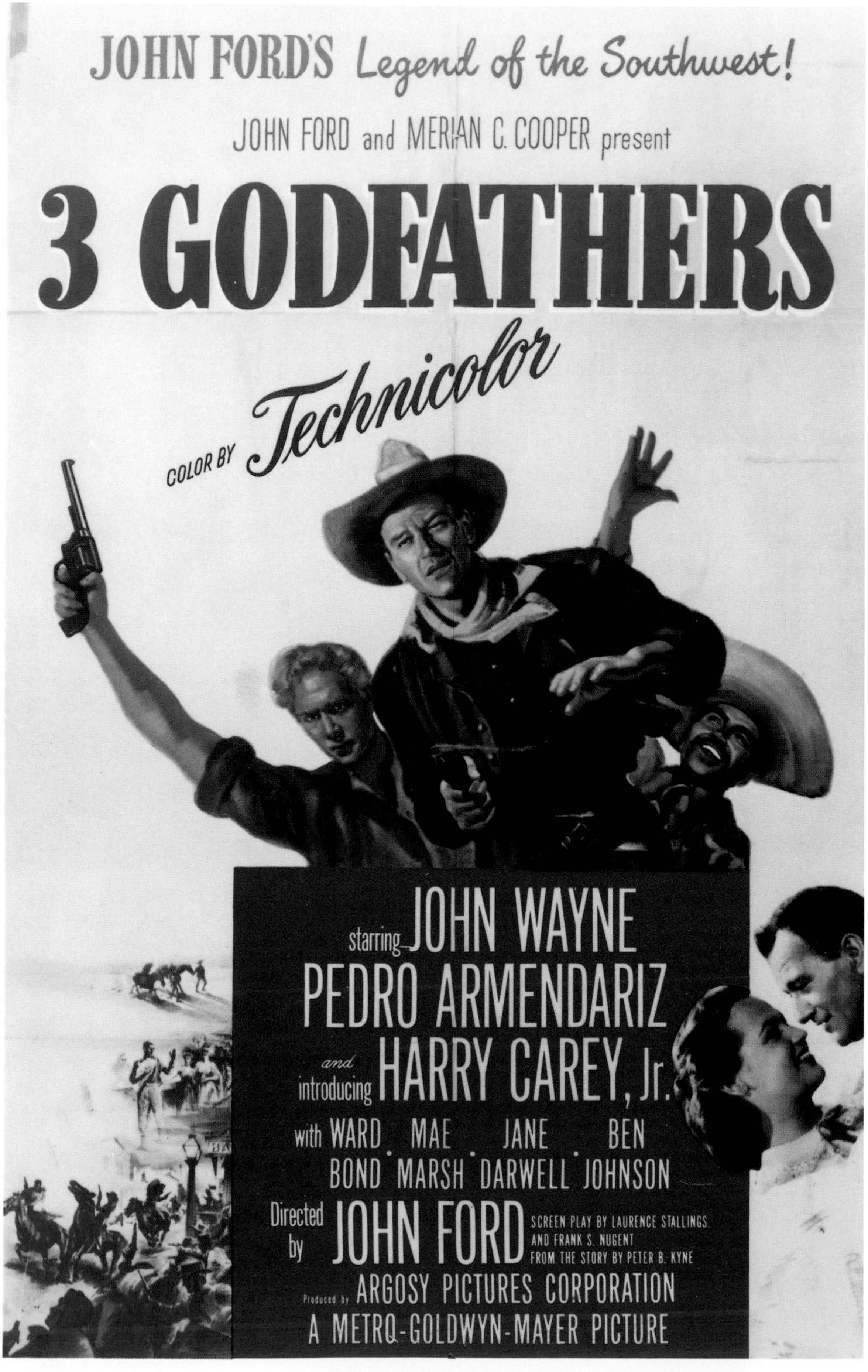
JOHN FORD'S Legend of the Southwest!
JOHN FORD and MERIAN C. COOPER present
3 GODFATHERS
COLOR BY Technicolor
starring JOHN WAYNE
PEDRO ARMENDARIZ
and introducing HARRY CAREY, Jr.
with WARD BOND . MAE MARSH . JANE DARWELL . BEN JOHNSON
Directed by JOHN FORD
SCREEN PLAY BY LAURENCE STALLINGS AND FRANK S. NUGENT
FROM THE STORY BY PETER B. KYNE
Produced by ARGOSY PICTURES CORPORATION
A METRO-GOLDWYN-MAYER PICTURE

Cary
GRANT
Loretta
YOUNG
David
NIVEN
in SAMUEL GOLDWYN'S
Cary and
The Bishop's Wife
RELEASED THROUGH RKO RADIO PICTURES INC.

Arnold Schwarzenegger directs the 1993 remake of *Christmas in Connecticut*, starring Dyan Cannon and Kris Kristofferson.

Hollywood Celebrates Christmas

Bette Davis

Judy Garland

Deanna Durbin

Alan Ladd

Shirley Temple

W.C. Fields and associates

Mack Sennett's Bathing Beauties

Ann-Margret

Mona Freeman

Carole Lombard

Kim Novak

Natalie Wood

Elizabeth Montgomery

Nancy Carroll

Mary Brian

Gene Tierney

Alice Faye

Edward G. Robinson
and Jane Wyman

Claude Jarman Jr.

Tuesday Weld

Paulette Goddard

"Our Gang"

Jayne Mansfield

Cary Grant

Christmas in Connecticut

BARBARA STANWYCK appeared in two classic Christmas movies that share certain characteristics besides their star—a homey, rural setting and a main character who isn't what she seems to be—but otherwise the films couldn't be less alike. *Remember the Night* (1940) is a beautiful, thoughtful, and often hilarious story of love and redemption, while *Christmas in Connecticut* is nothing more than a farce—an exceedingly well-performed and well-directed farce, but a mere farce nonetheless.

Christmas in Connecticut has the kind of plot that television situation comedy writers have mined for decades. If it's fresher than the variations that would come later, that has much to do with the glossy sheen of studio filmmaking, the bright direction by Peter Godfrey, and the irresistible performances by Stanwyck, Dennis Morgan, Reginald Gardiner, Sidney Greenstreet, and S. J. "Cuddles" Sakall. *Remember the Night* is memorable, funny, and touching. *Christmas in Connecticut* is only funny.

Stanwyck plays Elizabeth Lane, a magazine writer who has attracted a large following for her columns on cooking and living the perfect country family life—she's a kind of World War II-era Martha Stewart. Dennis Morgan plays Jefferson Jones, a war hero who was stranded on a life raft for weeks and who gave his last bit of food to his companion. Jones got through the ordeal by dreaming of food and of all the wonderful meals he would enjoy once he got home.

Barbara Stanwyck and Dennis Morgan in *Christmas in Connecticut*.

Someone gets the idea to have Jeff spend the Christmas holidays with Elizabeth, her husband, and her baby at the fabulous Connecticut farm about which she writes so persuasively; it would be great publicity for her magazine to show this kindness to a returning serviceman. The trouble is, everything about Elizabeth is a fake—she isn't married, doesn't have a baby, lives in a small Manhattan apartment, and can't cook. Faced with losing her job, she has no choice but to concoct the reality and to prepare for a nightmarish holiday with Jones, her overbearing boss (Greenstreet), a cafe owner Felix Bassenak (Sakall), who actually prepares all of her recipes, and John Sloan (Gardiner), the man who wants to marry her and conveniently owns a farm in Connecticut.

Christmas in Connecticut soon becomes one of those slamming-door farces, where everyone just barely escapes detection for the various frauds they are perpetrating. John has convinced Elizabeth to marry him and keeps summoning a good-natured judge (Dick Elliott) out to the farm to quickly perform the ceremony before the truth gets out. But once Elizabeth lays eyes on Jeff, all bets are off. She doesn't want to marry John but can't tell him for fear that he will expose the whole scheme.

Barbara Stanwyck and Dennis Morgan in *Christmas in Connecticut*.

There are moments of real humor and charm in the film, but *Christmas in Connecticut* is best when it allows itself to breathe a little, as when Jeff sings at the piano as Elizabeth decorates the Christmas tree or when the two take a moonlit sleigh ride across the snowy landscape.

Stanwyck said in 1988 that she particularly enjoyed making *Christmas in Connecticut* because "I didn't kill anyone in that picture! In spite of the fact that I've always loved to kill on-screen, it was a pleasant change of pace for me. It gave me another chance to do comedy."

Despite its title, Warner Bros. did not intend *Christmas in Connecticut* to be a Christmas release. In fact, it hit theaters in the middle of July 1945. Audiences responded well, but most critics saw through the cracks in the plot. "You might say there's never a dull moment," wrote Archer Winston in the *New York Post* (July 28, 1945), "and someone else might add with equal justice there's never a very good moment either."

On July 17, *Variety*'s critic wrote that the film "quick-steps through a series of quips, gags, and rollicking farce situations. Some of the latter are maybe none too plausible, but they are worked to the limit for laughs by writing, acting and directing. The sex motif is on a tightrope throughout, and constantly threatens to–but never quite does–topple into Hays office [censor] disfavor."

Although the reviews were mixed, the film was and remains a popular favorite. "It was a very relaxed project and I enjoyed participating in it," Stanwyck later said, "but never in my wildest dreams did I think it would be resurrected every holiday season! Obviously from the letters I've received, the public enjoyed it then and still does–*that* pleases me."

Christmas in Connecticut found its place as a Christmas movie on television. It's one of those warm, comfortable titles that show up every holiday season to be enjoyed with the same nostalgic pleasure as singing a Christmas carol or trimming the tree. This the kind of film whose appeal is so dependent upon the time in which it is made and the unique qualities of its actors, it would seem foolish to remake it.

So, of course, it was remade.

Not only was *Christmas in Connecticut* remade for television broadcast in 1992, it was directed by perhaps the least likely person for the job–Arnold Schwarzenegger.

This *Christmas in Connecticut* obviously had to make some changes in both plot and setting. Jefferson Jones (Kris Kristofferson) could no longer be a war hero–no war–so screenwriters Janet Brownell, Adele Commandini, Aileen Hamilton, and Lionel Houser turned him into a reclusive forest ranger who goes out into a Colorado blizzard to save a lost child. While he's performing the rescue, his cabin in the woods burns down. The only recognizable object left is a cookbook by Elizabeth Lane (Dyan Cannon).

Elizabeth is not a columnist as in the first version, but the host of a television cooking show. Like Stanwyck's Elizabeth, Cannon's can't cook and, indeed, has no domestic tendencies at all. This is the first problem of

Kris Kristofferson and Dyan Cannon in *Christmas in Connecticut* (1993).

plausibility in the film—you can believe a writer simply copying recipes and passing them off as her own. It is much harder to accept that someone who makes her living cooking on camera can't, in fact, cook. The character is not presented as a poor cook, or not quite what she's cracked up to be—Cannon's Elizabeth doesn't have the slightest clue how to do anything in the kitchen.

Her loud, aggressive producer, Alexander (Tony Curtis), finds out about the cookbook in Jeff's burned-out cabin and gets a brilliant idea: They'll invite Jeff to spend the holidays with Elizabeth for the purposes of doing a live broadcast from her home on Christmas Eve. Jeff, for his part, isn't quite sure who Elizabeth is and doesn't know where the cookbook came from, but he is offered $25,000 to appear on the broadcast—money he needs to rebuild his cabin—so he accepts.

Farce is a delicate thing. All is lost if the audience has time to stop and think, "Why are they going through all this? Why don't they just tell each other what's going on?" With *Christmas in Connecticut*, the audience starts thinking this immediately. Elizabeth hires her assistant, the one who really cooks for the show, and her psychotic actor husband to pretend to be her child, while Alexander steps in to pretend to be the husband, a role he wants in real life, too. The whole bunch start bickering from the first moments of the film and can barely even pretend to be a real family when Jeff arrives.

The problem with the plot is that there is really no reason to carry on the charade. In the original, Stanwyck's boss is also spending the holidays at the Connecticut farm, and she's afraid he'll fire her if he finds out she isn't what she's cracked up to be. But everyone in the remake knows that Cannon's Elizabeth is a fraud—everybody but Jeff, and he doesn't care. There is, consequently, no sense of danger to the charade. Once everybody finds out the truth, nothing substantially changes.

The live broadcast is, predictably, a shambles, simply because none of the participants can even pretend to cooperate, even as the cameras are rolling. Also, Elizabeth's assistant, for no good reason, goes out looking for Elizabeth and gets stuck in a snow drift—oh no! Who's going to do the cooking on live television?

The first *Christmas in Connecticut* is no masterpiece, but it is at least well made, amusing, and enjoyable. This remake is none of the above. Part of the blame can be laid on the superficial, joke-free script, and part—a big part—on the "direction" by Schwarzenegger. His idea of energy is to have everyone in the room scream at each other at the top of their lungs. And his idea of humor is to place at least two mocking references to himself in the film: one character puts on sunglasses at one point and says, Arnold style, "I'll be back!" and another character watches *Twins* (starring Schwarzenegger and Danny De Vito) on television.

The trouble is, those few seconds of *Twins* are more fun than anything in this miserable and implausible movie. *Christmas in Connecticut* offers its viewers an experience every bit as filled with tension, trauma, and unpleasantness as any of its characters live through, but without the happy ending they receive.

Miracle on 34th Street

Miracle on 34th Street is one of the most beloved of Christmas movies, a joyful and moving story about goodness and faith and our human need for fantasy. Beautifully directed by George Seaton, the film is also perfectly cast with Maureen O'Hara, John Payne, the adorable little Natalie Wood, and Edmund Gwenn as Kris Kringle, the man who claims to be the real Santa Claus—and who just might be.

As the film begins, Doris Walker (O'Hara) has to contend with a drunken Santa. She is personnel director for Macy's department store, and the Santa Claus who is supposed to provide the climax for the annual Thanksgiving Day Parade has taken in rather too much holiday cheer. Desperate for a replacement, she sees the perfect Santa. In fact, his name is Kris Kringle, and according to him, he not only looks like Santa, he *is* Old Saint Nick himself.

Impressed by his superb performance in the parade, Doris gives Kris a job at Macy's as the official toy department Santa. With his gentle demeanor and twinkling eyes, Kris proves to be perfect for that job, too. The kids who talk to him think that Kris must be the real thing—all the kids, that is, except Doris's pragmatic, illusion-free little daughter, Susan (Natalie Wood).

Miracle on 34th Street is not only about how Susan regains her faith in Santa Claus but also how all the people who come into contact with Kris have to examine their own beliefs. When he is put on trial to determine whether he is delusional and should be institutionalized, his lawyer Fred Gailey (Payne) and a perplexed Judge (Gene Lockhart) are faced with the possibility that Kris might be legally proven to be the true Santa Claus.

Mara Wilson as Susan Walker in *Miracle on 34th Street* (1994).

One of the qualities that immediately distinguishes *Miracle on 34th Street* from other Christmas or fantasy films is its air of documentary reality. Made in a postwar era that saw more location work for films that would have been made entirely in Hollywood before, *Miracle* was filmed in part on the actual streets of New York and in the real Macy's department store.

Originally titled *The Big Heart*, the film began production in late 1946. The company took over several floors of Macy's, which crowed proudly in its in-house organ, *The Macy Star*, that it was now "the first department store to be featured in a full length film production." (Take *that*, Gimbel's!) Director Seaton oversaw a crew of fourteen cameras on Thanksgiving Day in order to capture the entire parade on film.

The location shooting did wonders for the realistic look of the film, but it was rough going for eight-year-old Natalie Wood, who was contracted to appear both in *The Big Heart* and in that romantic ghost story *The Ghost and Mrs. Muir*, starring Gene Tierney and Rex Harrison. She had to fly back and forth between New York and Los Angeles at least once, and then, when the *Big Heart* company returned to the Hollywood studios of Twentieth Century-Fox, she had to be shuttled from set to set, making both movies at the same time—and affecting an English accent for *Ghost*. Little Natalie's performances in the two Fox films were considered so outstanding that the studio immediately arranged to buy out her current contract with Universal-International.

The release of *Miracle on 34th Street* was accompanied by what we would now call a "tie-in" book. The film was not based on the book, but vice versa. The original story by Valentine Davies had been adapted into screenplay

form by director George Seaton. Sometime during production of the movie, hoping to cheer up a sick friend,
Davies sent him a copy of the short story. Instead, the sick
friend cheered up Davies by giving the story to an
editor at a large publishing house who immediately
contracted Davies to adapt the story and screenplay into novel form. After getting permission from
Fox, Davies did just that—and got a best-seller out
of the deal.

Whimsy is perhaps the most difficult of qualities
to capture on film, another reason that *Miracle on
34th Street* is so special and so dear to generations
of viewers. As the *Newsweek* critic put it (June 2,
1947), "*Miracle* could have been all treacle and
bubble gum, and too cute for words; instead it is
the warm, human and delightfully amusing story of
an old gent who ... is fully convinced that he is
Santa Claus."

The film, in fact, was almost universally praised
by critics and loved by audiences. That love continues to this day when a screening of *Miracle on
34th Street* is an absolutely essential ingredient for
catching the holiday spirit.

Natalie Wood, Maureen O'Hara,
and John Payne star in *Miracle on
34th Street* (1947).

Given the place it holds in generations of
viewers' hearts, it might have seemed foolhardy to
attempt a remake, but, in fact,
there have been no less than
three new versions.

In 1955 *Miracle on 34th Street*
was produced as a live television
drama starring Don Beddoe,
Dick Foran, and Herb Vigran.
Television caught up with the
story again in 1973 with a made-
for-television movie directed by
Fielder Cook and starring Jane
Alexander as Karen (no longer
Doris) Walker, David Hartman
as her lawyer-love interest,
Roddy McDowell as psychiatrist
Henry Sawyer, and Sebastian
Cabot as Kris Kringle. Not as
bad as it might have been, this

In *Miracle on 34th Street* (1947), Kris Kringle (Edmund Gwenn)
lets Natalie Wood tug on his beard while John Payne
looks away.

television movie still missed the clear-eyed charm of the original by a country mile.

Producer John Hughes–whose forays into cinematic Christmas have included *Home Alone*, *Home Alone 2*, and *National Lampoon's Christmas Vacation*–came back to the story in the early nineties, determined to update it without losing the essential magic and emotion. Executive producer Bill Ryan said during production, "The film's themes are very dear to John. Faith, believing in people, and the meaning of Christmas, when people go out of their way to help each other. That spirit has been buried and downgraded by the modern commercialization of Christmas and it's important we bring it back."

Hughes's version, which was directed by Les Mayfield, stars Elizabeth Perkins as Dorey (not quite Doris) Walker; Dylan McDermott as Bryan Bedford, the lawyer whose name changes from film to film; Mara Wilson as Susan Walker; and Richard Attenborough as Kriss (not Kris) Kringle.

Like Seaton's original version, Hughes and Mayfield took the remake's company on location to New York to film the Thanksgiving Day Parade. Unlike Seaton, however, Mayfield did not film the real parade but, instead, recreated it on nine blocks of Central Park West, using two marching bands, four custom-made floats, helium balloons, and a sleigh pulled by eight reindeer and driven by Kriss.

Attenborough said later, "Nothing in all my years of acting compares to the feeling I had as I rode the Santa's sleigh float down Central Park West. It was an actor's dream of heaven. What was wonderful, and what this movie is about, is that I could see children in the crowd looking up to me with total belief as I went by. That gave me the most wonderful feeling of faith and love and trust."

After completing the New York filming, the company returned to Chicago, where Hughes always prefers to shoot and where virtually all of his films are set. The movie's department store Santa's Workshop was built in an empty, two-story ballroom at the School of the Art Institute of Chicago.

Although the new *Miracle* is set in present day, the costume and set designers made an effort to create a kind of timelessness to the clothes and locations. At one point, extras even had their ski jackets and other up-to-date duds replaced by classic wool coats to give them a slightly old-fashioned look.

The remake of *Miracle on 34th Street* turned out to be an excellent film in its own right. The situations are updated slightly without changing the basic nature of the plot, and although the outcome of Kriss's trial is the same in both films, the way they arrive at that point is quite different.

But the real treasure of the 1994 *Miracle* is Mara Wilson. She is as adorable as Natalie Wood but with a completely different personality–grave, old beyond her years. When she admits to Bryan that she knows "the secret"–that Santa Claus isn't real–she doesn't say it with cynicism but with real sadness, as though perfectly aware of what she has lost along with her childlike faith. Later, when Bryan takes her to the department store to meet Kriss, she doesn't believe that his beard is real, just as Natalie Wood's Susan doubted Edmund Gwenn's beard. When Natalie pulled it and realized it was the real thing, there was a look of quiet awe on her face, as if to say, "If I was wrong about this, what else might I be wrong about?" But when Mara pulls the beard and Kriss yelps, she has a look of pure delight. For a second–and for a change–she's a little girl talking to Santa Claus.

There is another magical moment of pure charm also involving a little girl and Santa. A little deaf girl is brought to Kriss by her mother who says, "You don't have to talk to her. She just wanted to meet you." But Kriss, who speaks every language, is equally fluent with American Sign Language and is soon entrancing the little girl with his conversation; they even sing a little carol together. Such a scene could be tastelessly maudlin; the fact that it is so filled with beauty and optimism and surprise is just one indication of how many things this movie got right.

Nothing will ever replace the original *Miracle on 34th Street*–it's one of the greatest of all great Christmas movies. But, against all expectations, the remake proves itself worthy of sitting right beside it on the video shelf, a real treat for, let's say, every *other* Christmas.

A musical remake of the classic 1947 motion picture stars Sabastion Cabot as an old man who professes to be–and well might be–the real Santa Claus in *Miracle on 34th Street* (1973).

Susan Walker (Mara Wilson), Dorey Walker (Elizabeth Perkins), Bryan Bedford (Dylan McDermott) in *Miracle on 34th Street* (1994).

It's a Wonderful Life (1946)

It's a Wonderful Life is perhaps the ultimate Christmas film, one of the most beloved movies ever made, and director Frank Capra's masterpiece. As small-town boy George Bailey, James Stewart essayed an Everyman for the ages, vastly broadening his scope as an actor. With a deep belief in the innate goodness of humanity, Capra created a modern fable that is by turns harrowing and hilarious, hopeful and grim. In it he explores some of his favorite themes—the triumph of good over bad, the strength of the individual, and the transforming power of love. *It's a Wonderful Life* is one of those rare movies that actually gets better with the passing years, achieving a cult status that belies its failure upon initial release.

Between 1934 and 1939, Capra had established himself as Hollywood's top director with a remarkable series of populist pictures. They were some of the highest-grossing films of the decade, winning Harry Cohn's Columbia Pictures two Oscars for Best Picture, for *It Happened One Night* (1934) and *You Can't Take It with You* (1938), and Capra three as Best Director, for *It Happened One Night*, *Mr. Deeds Goes to Town* (1936), and *You Can't Take It with You*. Capra faltered with his pretentious and overlong *Lost Horizon* (1937), and eventually his individualistic "one man, one film" approach to filmmaking brought him into conflict with studio mogul Cohn. After *Mr. Smith Goes to Washington* (1939), Capra took a lucrative deal at Warner, made an independent film (*Meet John Doe*) and a for-hire studio job (*Arsenic and Old Lace*), then became the U.S. government's leading propagandist with his World War II documentary series *Why We Fight*.

After the war, Capra was a different man, his trademark sentiment tempered with cynicism. Partnered with two other leading directors, William Wyler and George Stevens, he formed Liberty Films to gain total independence from the studio system. Liberty made a distribution deal with RKO, and Capra began searching for the right property. James Stewart, a fighter pilot in the air force, had undergone a similar transformation, emerging from the war with a dark side that had never been exploited on film. *It's a Wonderful Life* was the first postwar project for Capra and Stewart and reflects the darker concerns of both men.

Capra always claimed that the movie had its source in a Christmas card, but this recollection demeans the author, historian Philip Van Doren Stern, who wrote the original story "The Greatest Gift." Stern did send "The Greatest Gift" as a Christmas card, but it was a twenty-four-page short story not, in Capra's words, "a little Christmas card." In 1943, RKO acquired the story as a vehicle for Cary Grant and commissioned Dalton Trumbo, Clifford Odets, and Marc Connelly to write scripts. Capra bought the rights for $50,000 in September 1945 and worked on a new screenplay with the husband-and-wife team of Frances Goodrich and Albert Hackett. Michael Wilson

The citizens of Bedford Falls chip in to help George Bailey in *It's a Wonderful Life*.

wrote a subsequent draft, with Jo Swerling and Dorothy Parker doing uncredited polishes. Capra changed the name of Stern's protagonist from George Pratt to George Bailey and changed his occupation from a bank clerk to owner of a crumbling savings and loan association.

James Stewart stars as the troubled George Bailey in Frank Capra's *It's a Wonderful Life*.

The plot of *It's a Wonderful Life* is well known, intricately structured, and told in a series of extended flashbacks. It's Christmas Eve in the quintessential small town of Bedford Falls and people are praying for George Bailey (Stewart), who has lost his faith in himself–as well as a bundle of cash at Bailey Building and Loan. The prayers of wife Mary (Donna Reed), his children, mother (Beulah Bondi), and friends are heard in heaven, and the lovably inept angel, Clarence (Henry Travers), is dispatched to earth to save George from suicide. If successful, Clarence will finally earn his wings. He rises to his task. When George mutters, "I wish I'd never been born," Clarence shows him what the world would be like if he had never existed.

This alternate reality is a nightmarish vision of what could have been. George sees that he didn't stop the town druggist from accidentally poisoning a customer, that his wife became a loveless spinster, and that Bedford Falls degenerated into a hub of sin and corruption, named Pottersville after evil rich man Potter (Lionel Barrymore). Clarence shows George the grave of his brother Harry, dead at age nine since George didn't save him; consequenty Harry didn't grow up to be a war hero, saving the lives of hundreds of men on a transport ship. ("Harry wasn't there to save them because you weren't there to save Harry. You see, George, you really had a wonderful life. Don't you see what a mistake it would be to throw it away?") George realizes his blessings, and in an ending that defines "Capraesque," he is blissfully reunited with family and friends, who pool their resources to save his business while singing "Auld Lang Syne." Unashamedly sentimental, it can still move an audience to tears of joy.

The cast of *It's a Wonderful Life* was richly populated

with some of the greatest character actors in Hollywood history, many of whom were Capra regulars–Thomas Mitchell as absent-minded Uncle Billy, Beulah Bondi as George's saintly mother, Ward Bond as Bert the cop, Frank Faylen as Ernie the taxi driver, H. B. Warner as Mr. Gower the druggist, Lionel Barrymore as evil Old Man Potter, and Henry Travers as Clarence the angel. Donna Reed made a perfect all-American wife, while Gloria Grahame provided sex appeal as the flirtatious Violet Bick.

For his Hollywood homecoming film, Capra pulled out all the stops, lavishing a $3 million budget on the picture. The quaint little burg of Bedford Falls was built from scratch on the RKO Ranch in Encino, Calfornia, with a Main Street spanning three city blocks. Filming began on April 15, 1946; after eighty-eight days of shooting, the picture was completed on July 27, ready for editing and music scoring and a 1946 Christmas release.

"No man is a failure who has friends"–that's the message of *It's a Wonderful Life*. But it was a message that postwar audiences didn't want to hear. Capra had become too Capracsque for his own good. The top-grossing pictures of 1946 were Wyler's drama of returning servicemen, *The Best Years of Our Lives*; the lust-in-the-dust Western *Duel in the Sun*; and the nostalgic music of *Blue Skies* and *The Jolson Story*. *It's a Wonderful Life* was a resounding flop, and Capra's career never fully recovered. Jimmy Stewart, on the other hand, rose to greater heights, as the addled Elwood P. Dowd in *Harvey* and as a neurotic hero in Anthony Mann's Westerns and Alfred Hitchcock's thrillers.

But in the early seventies, a strange phenomenon occurred. New generations discovered the delights of *It's a Wonderful Life* through repeated television broadcasts. The film had slipped into the abyss of the public domain; television stations played it endlessly without having to pay a license fee, and in the eighties the picture became available from a dozen different home video distributors. *It's a Wonderful Life* became a national treasure, and Capra, in his old age, was toasted by film students and movie buffs. John McDonough, writing in *The Wall Street Journal* (December 19, 1984), observed that "*It's a Wonderful Life* has quietly replaced Charles Dickens' *A Christmas Carol* as the Great American Christmas Story."

Lionel Barrymore as the evil Mr. Potter in *It's A Wonderful Life*. Also starring James Stewart (*right*).

Marlo Thomas, Cloris Leachman, Wayne Rogers, and Orson Welles star in the ill-conceived remake of *It's a Wonderful Life*, *It Happened One Christmas*.

In 1977 the unthinkable happened–*It's a Wonderful Life* was remade for television; to purists, this was akin to remaking *Citizen Kane*. The ABC telefilm *It Happened One Christmas* switched the characters' genders, with Marlo Thomas in the Jimmy Stewart role, Wayne Rogers in the Donna Reed part, and Cloris Leachman as the angel, renamed Clara. Orson Welles co-starred as Potter. Not only was the remake a bad idea, at 150 minutes, it was 20 excruciating minutes longer than the original.

J. A. G.

The Bishop's Wife (1947) and *The Preacher's Wife* (1996)

The Bishop's Wife is a Christmas story of divine intervention.

Rev. Henry Brougham (David Niven), an Episcopal bishop, is plagued with troubles. Overworked and underappreciated, he is desperate to raise funds to build a spectacular new cathedral. To accomplish this goal, he must kowtow to his parish's richest snobs, particularly a wealthy widow who intends to fund the project as a garish monument to her late husband.

The cathedral project takes all of Henry's time, energy, and attention, leaving little for his wife, Julia (Loretta Young), and daughter, Debby (Karolyn Grimes, Zuzu from *It's a Wonderful Life*). Clearly, Henry needs help. And he gets it, in the form of a dapper angel named Dudley (Cary Grant) who shows up precisely when he's needed most–at Christmas.

Monty Wooley, Loretta Young, and Cary Grant as Dudley the angel in *The Bishop's Wife.*

Based on the 1928 novel by Robert Nathan (who also wrote that gossamer fantasy *Portrait of Jenny*), *The Bishop's Wife* is about a marriage that has lost its magic only to have it restored by a magic being. Dudley does not accomplish his goals by simply waving an angelic wand and causing miracles; rather, he subtly manipulates everyone to find their own solutions to life's problems. His attention is flattering to the lonely Julia, who begins to feel girlish and happy again. But that same attention causes Henry to develop an intense jealousy, an emotion that makes him view his wife with new eyes and serves to revive his passion for her.

Dudley also works his magic with the agnostic Professor Wutheridge (Monty Wooley), by inspiring him to once again take up his long-neglected book on Roman history, and with the rich widow Mrs. Hamilton (Gladys Cooper), by making her realize that her single-minded zeal to build the cathedral comes not out of love for her husband but from her enduring guilt that she actually loved another man. Dudley is more counselor than wizard, although he can come up with a doozy of a trick when he wants. He can decorate a Christmas tree, file papers, or type a letter with a simple gesture. He gets the neighborhood kids to accept Debby in their snowball fight by giving her a powerful and accurate pitching arm. And when Henry visits Mrs. Hamilton and

Cary Grant, Sarah Haden, and David Niven in *The Bishop's Wife*.

is in danger of submitting to her wishes once again, Dudley sticks Henry to a chair, making sure that he remains there for hours.

One of the reasons that *The Bishop's Wife* is so enduringly effective is that Dudley is not a high-minded angel, but one who longs for the life he once knew on earth and for the sensual pleasures he can no longer share. He intends to arouse Henry's jealousy to revive Henry's love for Julia; what he doesn't count on is that he will fall in love with Julia himself, and she with him. This turn of the plot gives the film a surprising depth of emotion that it would lack if it were only a fantasy about a Christmas angel who works miracles. For when Dudley wipes clean the memory of everyone who has met him and moves on to his next assignment, it is with a genuine sense of loss and pain—emotions that we don't expect angels to possess.

Because of the charm of the cast, the skill of director Henry Koster and the beautiful and witty simplicity of the script by Robert E. Sherwood and Leonardo Barcovici, the film never descends into the maudlin or the precious. It's moving and romantic, yes, but also wonderfully funny.

The production was none of those things. Most of those

involved, in fact, remember it as a kind of prolonged nightmare.

In 1946 the Samuel Goldwyn production was about to go before the cameras with Teresa Wright as the title character and David Niven as the angel Dudley; they were to be directed by William A. Seiter. Filming was just about to start when Theresa Wright, who had completed all of her wardrobe fittings, learned that pretty soon the wardrobe would no longer fit–she was pregnant.

Goldwyn replaced her with Loretta Young, whom he borrowed from RKO along with Cary Grant. The producer felt that they would be perfect as the bishop and his wife. After three weeks of production–and an expenditure of close to a million dollars–Goldwyn realized he had made a mistake. Seiter wasn't catching the proper tone of whimsical fantasy that the story required. The actors were unhappy, Goldwyn was unhappy, and Seiter was soon out of a job. Goldwyn also had all the sets torn down and rebuilt.

The producer called Henry Koster, who had made his mark at Universal in the thirties and early forties with a series of highly profitable Deanna Durbin vehicles such as *Three Smart Girls* (1936), *First Love* (1939), and *It Started with Eve* (1941). Koster was a true actor's director, with a deft hand at comedy and a light touch with sentiment.

"[Goldwyn] took me into the projection room," Koster said later, "and ran some of the film put together already. In the first version, David Niven played the angel and Cary was the bishop. Goldwyn said, 'That's wrong to cast them that way, because David Niven would be a much better bishop and Cary Grant would be a much better angel.' I said, 'Yes, but then the script will have to be slightly adjusted to do that.' He said, 'You go to New York and work with the author, Robert Sherwood, on the script and do what you think should be done.'"

Switching Niven and Grant in the roles made everyone happy except Cary Grant. Grant begged Goldwyn to reconsider. "You want me to be happy, don't you?" he asked the producer. Goldwyn replied, "You are going to be here for only a few weeks and this picture will be out a long time. I would rather you be unhappy here, and then we can all be happy later."

Although Koster later said he "loved doing that picture," he also admitted that Grant's displeasure with playing the angel made for some tense moments on the set: "This is the worst thing that can happen to a director, to work with an actor who doesn't want to play a part, and has to do it."

The director had another problem with his stars. Both Cary Grant and Loretta Young were convinced that they were only photogenic on the left side of their faces, and both insisted that only this side be photographed. Koster tried to accommodate this phobia as long as he could, but finally he came to a love scene—if both actors wanted to stress the same profile, how could they face each other for a love scene?

Koster said, "I did some rearranging of the scene, and had her step up and look out the window. Then I had him step behind her and put his hands on her shoulder and lean his cheek to her ear, so they were both looking out the window. I had two profiles in the same direction. Then they had that romantic dialog."

When Goldwyn saw the footage, he exploded with anger. He called Koster into his office and bawled him out. Koster tried to explain things. So Goldwyn stormed down to the soundstage and approached Grant and Young. He told them in no uncertain terms that there would be no such nonsense in the future. "I'll tell you one thing," Goldwyn said. "From now on both of you get only half of your salary if I can only use half of your face!"

The Bishop's Wife was intended to open during the Christmas season of 1947, but it almost missed its opening date when preview audiences didn't much care for the film. Goldwyn brought in Billy Wilder and Charles Brackett to write a few new scenes; these additions must have done the trick because the result was a hit at the box office and the recipient of rave reviews. "It is superb," wrote the *The New York Times*'s Bosley Crowther, "and it comes close to being the most enchanting picture of the year."

The film also garnered several Academy Award nominations: picture, director, musical score (Hugo Friedhofer), and film editing (Monica Collingwood). The only Oscar that *The Bishop's Wife* took home was for sound recording (the Goldwyn Sound Department). The Academy Award for Best Actress did go to Loretta Young that year—for *The Farmer's Daughter*.

other Georgia cities and towns. In most musical sequences in movies, all the singing is prerecorded, then later lip-synched by the performers during the production. But to preserve the excitement of this music, Houston decided that all the singing would be recorded live for the cameras.

One night, while filming at Trinity United Methodist Church in Newark, New Jersey, Houston and the choir got so involved in their music that they just wouldn't stop singing, no matter how many times Marshall yelled, "Cut!"

"I just kept the camera rolling," the director said. "We loaded magazine after magazine of the film as if we were shooting a documentary. It was dizzying."

Houston said later that the impromptu concert was a release after working so hard, for so long. "I truly believe the Holy Spirit came down and took over," she said, "because I saw people on the set—people you never dreamed would be touched—crying and sobbing."

In addition to the Newark location, *The Preacher's Wife* searched out appropriate winter spots in Portland, Maine; Lake Success, New York; Yonkers, New York; and Jersey City, New Jersey. The wintry weather essential to the story's mood turned out to be something of a nightmare for the filmmakers. The very first day of shooting in Yonkers was delayed because the Blizzard of '96 had dumped thirty inches of snow on the area. "We could not get in," Marshall told a reporter. "We offered to bring our own trucks in to plow the area we needed to shoot in [outside] this courthouse. They said no. So already we were a day behind. The next day, it took eight hours to clear out the snow and get the set dressed."

When the company moved up to Portland, Maine, to shoot an ice skating sequence on a frozen pond, they found the weather to be rainy and warm. "So now all the snow is off the hills and there's three inches of water on the ice," Marshall said, "and it's melting." They had to use artificial ice to dress the scene, and the cast members were sweltering in their winter clothes. Marshall said that she was forced to film from one angle only to retain the snowy look. "It's getting slushier," she recalled, "and there were little holes in the ice that we were filling in. By the third day, we were stuck in one little corner and it was unsafe to go on the ice."

While in Yonkers, some offscreen drama took everyone's attention away from the set. An apartment building caught fire near the church where they were filming. One technician climbed a ladder to a second-story window and rescued a four-year-old boy, whose younger brother and sister died in the blaze. Ironically, their mother described the lost children as "sweet, beautiful angels."

Although both versions of this story are set at Christmas, *The Preacher's Wife* exploits the imagery of the season more than *The Bishop's Wife* does. In addition to some of the seasonal music performed by Houston and the choir, there is a lovely children's Christmas pageant in which the Baby Jesus is played by a wetting doll that chooses a moment in the middle of the show to wet on the Virgin Mary. Her abrupt departure from the stage leads to a last minute substitution by Houston, who sings a special Christmas song with the children.

For her bravura performance as Julia, Houston won an Image Award as Outstanding Lead Actress in a Motion Picture. Her fellow actors, Loretta Devine, Jenifer Lewis, and Justin Pierre Edmund, were also nominated for Image Awards. *The Preacher's Wife* received a single Oscar nomination, for Hans Zimmer's musical score.

But perhaps the biggest triumph of *The Preacher's Wife* is that it didn't destroy the gentle magic of the earlier film that inspired it. One critic called *The Preacher's Wife* "sweetly uplifting," and the fact that a movie made in 1996 could be so described is a little miracle in and of itself. It may not ever become the revered classic that *The Bishop's Wife* is, but *The Preacher's Wife* is a warm and inspiring film—funny and touching and, yes, "sweetly uplifting." And that is everything a great Christmas movie needs to be.

Come to the Stable (1949)

IN THE OPENING moments of *Come to the Stable*, two nuns walk across a wintry landscape of storybook beauty. The pure white snow glistens under twinkling stars and an angelic chorus fills the soundtrack with sweet and haunting sounds. The nuns, Sister Margaret (Loretta Young) and Sister Scholastica (Celeste Holm), pause to

Celeste Holm, Loretta Young, and Elsa Lanchester in *Come to the Stable*.

look at a road sign that points toward Jordan, Galilee, Nazareth, and Bethlehem. They smile with satisfaction; this must be the place.

Drawn by the pure soprano of a young boy singing "Adeste Fideles"–in Latin–the Sisters approach a brightly lit stable nestled in a snowy valley. Inside they find a carefully composed Nativity scene. Joseph, Mary, and a shepherd, joined by a sheep and a cow, gaze in wonderment at the baby in the manger. Standing to one side are two angels–two small boys, one of whom is singing the carol. Hanging overhead is a third angel, obviously sick of being suspended from ropes. One of the angels on the ground is sick, too, sick of the other's singing. He kicks his older brother in the shin.

Celeste Holm and Loretta Young in *Come to the Stable*.

Sisters Margaret and Scholastica now know for certain they're in the right place. They have traveled all the way from France to find this stable-turned-artist's studio.

More specifically, they have come to see the artist, Miss Potts (Elsa Lanchester), an eccentric woman who specializes in religious paintings.

The American cinema of 1949 was distinguished by great war pictures such as William Wellman's *Battleground* and Henry King's *Twelve O'clock High*, cynical dramas like Robert Rossen's *All The King's Men*, and tough films noir like Mark Robson's *Champion*. But from the first moments of *Come to the Stable*, it was clear to audiences that they were in a world in which cynicism, cruelty, violence, and darkness had no place. Instead, it is a world in which even the worst people have good characteristics just waiting to be brought to the surface, where sacrifice and charity and faith are prevalent. In short, *Come to the Stable* is not much like real life, and it certainly isn't much like any other film of its time.

Sisters Margaret and Scholastica have come to Bethlehem—a tiny town in New England—to fulfill a vow. During the war, their children's hospital in France had been in danger of being bombed. Sister Margaret prayed that if God spared the hospital, she would some day come to America and build another like it. Her prayer was answered; although the entire town was leveled, her hospital was saved. "God fulfilled his part of the bargain," she tells Miss Potts, "and now I'm going to try and fulfill mine." Their quest to find the money and support needed to build the hospital takes them to the area's bishop, a feared crime boss, and a jazz composer with a yen for solitude. Needless to say, each of these adversaries falls before the simple faith of the two nuns, and the hospital is about to be built as the film ends.

There is no danger of spoiling the film by revealing the ending; no viewer could have the slightest doubt how things are going to turn out. The pleasure in the film is in the beautifully modulated performances, the charming, literate script, and the inspirational music of Cyril Mockridge and Alfred Newman. It makes for perfect Christmas viewing, even though Christmas isn't really the subject, or even the background, of the film. After the opening scenes with its glittering stars, snowy hills, and poignant manger scene, there is no more reference to Christmas. But the texture of goodness, hope, and answered prayers make this a rare film of religious meaning and sentimental tenderness, just right for holiday viewing.

Its religious aspect almost caused the film not to be made. Darryl Zanuck, head of Twentieth Century-Fox, wanted Loretta Young to star in a comedy called *Mother Is a Freshman*, about a mother and daughter who attend college together and end up in love with the same man. "I said, 'I don't care about that,'" Loretta Young told an interviewer, "'but you do have a story on the shelf that I would love to do. It's called *Come to the Stable*.' They told me they didn't want to make it because it was a religious story. But I kept on about it, and finally they said, 'Okay, we'll do *Come to the Stable* if you'll do *Mother Is a Freshman* first.'" She balked at the compromise, but her agent, Myron Selznick, pointed out to her that the studio wanted to sign her for two pictures at once. Young said there was just one more condition before she would agree: "I want roses in my dressing room," she told Selznick. She said later, "Darryl had never sent me flowers in all the years I'd been with [Twentieth Century-Fox]. So I got my roses and they got their two pictures. Both pictures were most successful. I'm happy to say that *Come to the Stable* was more successful and still is. They play it every year on TV."

Come to the Stable is a masterpiece of the type of studio filmmaking that has now become virtually obsolete. The rolling New England hills, roads and rustic church and farmhouse were all built on two huge soundstages. One of them was ringed by a giant cyclorama that covered more than 60,000 square feet and allowed the camera to turn 360 degrees. The home of the musician, played by Hugh Marlowe, was actually the eight-acre Henry Fonda estate in Brentwood, California; the home's exteriors and interiors were used, as were the guest houses and tennis courts.

The director of *Come to the Stable* was Henry Koster who, the year before, had directed Loretta Young, Cary Grant, and David Niven in another great Christmas movie, *The Bishop's Wife*. Responsible for many delightful films with Deanna Durbin and classics like *Harvey* (1950) with James Stewart, Koster was drawn to religious subjects several times over the course of his career. In addition to *The Bishop's Wife* and *Come to the*

Stable, Koster directed a biography of evangelist Peter Marshall, *A Man Called Peter* (1955); *The Story of Ruth* (1960); and the first film released in CinemaScope, *The Robe* (1953). Koster's last film was the popular—if saccharine—*The Singing Nun* (1966), starring Debbie Reynolds.

"I was always very much interested in religion, and I still am," Koster told an interviewer. "I'm the only Jew, I think, who goes regularly to church. I've never been to temples, but then I wasn't brought up that way. I think [*Come to the Stable*] had a religious feeling, even more than *The Bishop's Wife*."

The original story was written by Clare Booth Luce, but Koster "never had the pleasure of working with" her. "When I was assigned to the picture," he said, "she had already written the first draft. Then the final polish was done by Sally [Benson]. The story was that those two [nuns] seemed to perform miracles without knowing how. They weren't really miracles. They were very practical things that happened and helped them solve their problems. It was like a little nun fairy tale."

Come to the Stable was a moderate box-office hit, much to the surprise of the Twentieth Century-Fox executives who only grudgingly allowed it to be produced. It was well reviewed, too: *The Hollywood Reporter* (June 22, 1949) wrote that the film "has the kind of enchanting force that will prove irresistible both as entertainment and a box office attraction. It is simply a lovely picture with a story as plain as the nose on one's face, but it is done with consummate taste, rare good humor and a wonderfully frothy disposition."

Variety (June 22, 1949) agreed, citing the film's "top-notch production and technical talent," its "inspired acting," and its "heart and understanding. The combined results spell touching and beautiful entertainment that will be understood and enjoyed by both masses and classes."

Come to the Stable was rewarded with several Academy Award nominations for Best Actress (Loretta Young), Best Supporting Actress (Celeste Holm), Best Story (Clare Booth Luce), Best Black-and-White Cinematography (Joseph LaShelle), Best Art Direction (Lyle Wheeler and Joseph C. Wright) and Set Decoration (Thomas Little and Paul S. Fox), and Best Song ("Through a Long and

Loretta Young stars in *Come to the Stable*.

Sleepless Night," music by Alfred Newman, lyrics by Mack Gordon).

Better still, it has become a staple of the Christmas season on television, where, every year, new viewers are introduced to its world of beauty, faith, and hopeful sweetness. *Come to the Stable* does not resemble any real life, past or present. But it's a world that is inordinately pleasant and moving to live in for a couple of warm Christmas hours.

A Christmas Story (1983): An Oral History

WHEN MOST PEOPLE are asked to name their favorite Christmas movies, the list includes *It's a Wonderful Life*, *The Bishop's Wife*, *Miracle on 34th Street*, *A Christmas Carol*—all classics from the thirties and forties. But in the last few years, a more recent film has joined that list— indeed, it seems to have gone straight to the head of the line as everybody's number-one Christmas film—*A Christmas Story*, written and narrated by Jean Shepherd and directed by Bob Clark.

A Christmas Story is a nearly plotless film about the Parker family of Cleveland, Ohio. Set vaguely in the forties, it centers around the family's preparations for Christmas. More specifically, it's about Ralphie Parker's single-minded obsession for his dream Christmas present—a Genuine Red Ryder Carbine Action Two Hundred Shot Lightning Loader Range Model Air Rifle with a Shock-Proof High Adventure Combination Trail Compass and Sundial set in the stock. To Ralphie, this BB gun is the center of his universe, the only thing worthy of his aspirations. But whenever he mentions it to any adult—even a department store Santa—he always gets the same deflating response: "You'll shoot your eye out."

A Christmas Story is hilarious, nostalgic, touching, and cynical—often all at the same time. Its meandering structure allows numerous little side stories—the Old Man (Darren McGavin) wins a "major award," a garish lamp shaped like a woman's leg; one of Ralphie's pals, Flick (Scott Schwartz), gets "double dog dared" to stick his tongue to a frozen light pole; and Ralphie confronts bullies, uncomprehending teachers, and a highly disappointing *Little Orphan Annie* decoder ring. But nobody watches *A Christmas Story* for plot; it's treasured for its great moments of humor, Ralphie's fantasies of BB gun greatness, and its perfectly realized atmosphere of Christmas with the family.

Only a marginal success in its original release, *A Christmas Story* has since become nearly a cult film on home video and television. During the Christmas season of 1996, the cable channel Turner Network Television (TNT) picked one day and played it over and over—all day long. Consequently, this is one Christmas movie that needs no introduction. Here, some of the people who made the movie—writer Jean Shepherd, director Bob Clark, and actors Peter Billingsley and Darren McGavin—describe the production of *A Christmas Story* and ponder why it has been so thoroughly embraced by moviegoers everywhere.

Getting Started:

BOB CLARK: *A Christmas Story* is a collection of Jean Shephard's short stories, published in *Playboy*; and his book, *Wanda Hickey*; and his other anthology stories. And [it's] also taken directly from his stage act at Princeton college, where he sat for two hours and mesmerized college students by just telling these tales. So it was an amalgam of Jean Shepherd tales.

JEAN SHEPHERD: Well, it came from a novel called *In God We Trust—All Others Pay Cash*. And it was funny. A couple of the newspapers in New York called it an American comedy classic. It was a very funny novel. And the first chapter in that novel was what later became *A Christmas Story*. It starts out with this kid waiting in line to see Santa Claus. You don't know why he is doing this, but he's standing there waiting to see Santa Claus. And before you finish reading the story, you realize he didn't want to see Santa Claus at all. He wants a BB gun. And he figures this is

Melinda Dillon as the mother, Darren McGavin as 'The Old Man,' Ian Petrella as Randy, and Peter Billingsley as Ralphie in *A Christmas Story*.

one way to get it. He wasn't hip on Christmas, but he was sure hip on BB guns, the Red Ryder BB gun in fact, and that's how it started. And it appeared in *Playboy* and won an award for the funniest humor in *Playboy* that year. A big cause célèbre that story was. But the actual name of the story was "The Red Ryder Plugs the Cleveland Street Kid."

BOB CLARK: *A Christmas Story* was spawned ten years before I ever got to do it. I was driving through Miami to Coral Gables, Florida, to pick up a date. And I heard this man on the radio, who I didn't know, Jean Shepherd it turned out to be, telling a story about the little boy who gets his tongue stuck to the light pole, frozen. I said, "God, I got to hear the end of this. I'll just go around the block a couple times." Well, Jean takes forty-five minutes to tell that story alone. So forty-five minutes later, with a very irate date, I said to myself, "I'm going to make a movie of this man's work." Little did I know that that was just the very beginning of the richness of Jean Shephard's work. So I started pursuing it, and within a year, I got him to agree with me and that was like 1973 or '74. And ten years later, in '83 we finally got some money, only because *Porky's* was a giant hit.

JEAN SHEPHERD: I'm sure when Herman Melville finished writing *Moby Dick*, two guys jumped out of the bushes and asked if he's got a movie deal. I wasn't that interested in doing it as a movie because it was a book and it was a well-received book. In today's world, it's most important to get a movie. A movie is more important than anything. I mean, that's why the Bible is not popular any more. It was really never made into a serious movie. So, anyway, when Bob showed up, I knew Bob vaguely because Bob's lawyer was also a friend of a lawyer that I was going to at the time. And anyway, Bob called me and said, "You know, I'd like to talk to you about making a movie." And I said, "Well, that's a great idea, Bob." Now the one thing I knew about Bob was that Bob really did do things. He wasn't a wanna-be. Bob was a real working guy. He did a movie. He did it and moved on to the next deal. So he calls me and says how about making a movie. And I said, well, terrific, come on out to the house. So he did. And in the meantime, I had started to put together a script for such a movie. Bob had said that he'd like to do the first chapter in the book; he thought it was a very funny story. And so he said, there isn't a male alive who hasn't been told by a female relative, usually his mother, "You'll shoot your eye out, kid," whenever you ask for a BB gun. So he thought it was funny.

Bob came over and we talked. And the next thing you know, we made a loose agreement that we were going to do a movie. And that I was going to do the script, but I also stipulated to

Bob, that it's to be done in a specific style, Bob, or it's not going to be funny. It's got to be funny. It's not nostalgic. It's funny. So Bob said, "Yeah." I said, "Well, you're gonna agree [with] me then that I'm going to be involved in working with you in the direction this movie's going to take." And he said, "Absolutely." Because in those days he respected me.

We started to work, and a couple of years later after a lot of dealing with various movie companies, we finally got the money for it, at M-G-M. And we started to do it. And we really went from that minute on, we just never stopped.

Writing the Script:

BOB CLARK: It was full collaboration. It's all Jean's original characters and situations basically. I probably contributed more to the narration, oddly enough, than I did to anything else. The dialog is taken directly from [Shepherd's original] material. It was a collaboration between Jean and his wife, Lee, and me.

JEAN SHEPHERD: No. The script was actually done by me and by my wife, Lee Brown, who's also given credit on that movie as a cowriter. She and I worked together on the script, and Bob liked it and enjoyed it very much. That's the way it went.

Autobiographical Elements:

BOB CLARK: I grew up in Birmingham, Alabama. Birmingham's a steel town the same as Hammond is. Indiana's on the edge of Chicago steel. So the flavor or the feeling of the piece is kind of autobiographical. It's earlier than my time, but still the fifties weren't that different from the late thirties and early forties, which is the mythical setting of *Christmas Story*. I had a tremendous identification with the piece. I later found out a tremendous number of people did, too.

DARREN MCGAVIN: It didn't really strike an autobiographical chord with me. Not really. The characters are very different; the old man was nothing like my father, so I had no reference in that area at all. And one deals with what the pages are, you know, the script. I arrived there, put on my wardrobe, and went to work.

JEAN SHEPHERD: Oh, yeah. I think any writer, especially if you write so much about childhood things, can't help but bring some experiences that he had as a kid. You can't invent a childhood, unless you're writing *Alice in Wonderland*. So, yeah, it's autobiographical, but a lot of it isn't. The kid was much tougher in the original novel. He was a tough little guy. He wasn't that little–he went on to become an athlete in high school, worked in the steel mill and so forth, so he wasn't a little namby-pamby kid.

Peter Billingsley:

BOB CLARK: Peter Billingsley–I think he actually was the very first child I saw. And after that, well, I've got to go and see thousands [of children] and I did. We went to every city, but he never got out of my mind totally. And I finally brought him back and I said, "What am I doing?" Yeah, he's obvious. Yeah, it's right on the nose, because he's it. And he's as imaginative and inventive and fresh a little guy as I've ever seen. So he was fated.

PETER BILLINGSLEY: At that point in my career when I got the role in *Christmas Story*, I had been working since I was about two and a half. And so it sort of came up like an audition, not unlike hundreds of others, and I went through a big process where you audition and read for the casting director. And then [I] was told that I was being considered and I didn't hear anything. And a month and a half went by, and [I] was called up to Canada to do a screen test. And so that in itself sounded like a lot of fun. So I packed my bags with my mom and we flew up north to Toronto and they sort of do a big paring process where they had maybe from my five guys from my row and five for all the others and they mix and match and it was a day and a half affair. And towards the end of the final day and a half, I was exhausted and had been through everything, and I was kind of one of the last guys left standing. And Bob said to me right then, he said, "Congratulations, you've got the role." And that's actually the only time that's ever happened. Because generally there's this big waiting process and a negotiating process, but Bob told me right on the spot that, in fact, I had gotten the role.

JEAN SHEPHERD: I thought Peter was marvelous in it. I thought he was great. I was surprised. We picked Peter up as a result of a commercial we saw that he did. Messy Marvin was the name of the kid in this commercial. And he just looked right, and so we read him for it, and he was right. He was the perfect, perfect kid for the movie.

DARREN MCGAVIN: It was just all such a wonderful experience with Peter. He's such a delightful young man. He truly is. He's now about twenty-three years old, and he's a remarkable child.

BOB CLARK: Jean didn't want to be too much involved in the casting. He kind of came in at the last and saw. Liked them all and felt the choices were good. And [he] hung around for a while, and I think he found it kind of frustrating to have to sit on the side and watch. I think he was there about half the time, but then of course came back for post production and posed and he was very pleased. He was very happy with what he saw.

PETER BILLINGSLEY: Jean had a lot to do with production. Jean was on the set constantly and it was funny because Jean had written the piece and it was so near and dear to his heart, obviously, that he...there were certain ways that he wanted things done. And frequently, Bob would be trying to set up a shot and saying, "All right, Peter, I want you to do it this way, and it's just the way we talked about." And Bob would sort of go off to the rest room and Jean would come diving in and say, "No. No. No. This doesn't make any sense." And then Bob would come out of the rest room and he would catch Jean and then they would sort of squabble. I think both their hearts were so in the project and so much invested that they ultimately wanted the best product possible and it all seemed to click.

BOB CLARK: Yeah. I think that was one of Jean's frustrations. He had to find out very quickly that it was almost impossible for two of us to—I didn't say much, but basically the boy is going to

Ralphie (Peter Billingsley), Schwartz (R.D. Robb), and friends cringe after Flick (Scott Schwartz) takes a dare to put his tongue on a frozen pole in *A Christmas Story*.

do what the director says. That's where the bond was. So it wasn't a problem for me. It was a little bit for Peter. But yeah, I remember that.

JEAN SHEPHERD: Did I tell Peter how to play his part? No, his mother tends to be protective. You know, the minute he's through, they whip him into the limo, pull him out and he's back in the hotel and you don't see him until the next day. So you—you don't spend much time with a kid like that.

DARREN MCGAVIN: Jean? Oh, he was there for the first few days. Yeah, he was there in the department store sequence at the top. And a couple of more days, and then he went back to Florida.

PETER BILLINGSLEY: The role was complicated in that there was not a lot of dialogue. And so much of it was what was going on in Ralphie's head, which was the narration read by Jean Shepherd. So I think he needed an actor who was able to react a lot. And for some reason that seemed to be sort of my forte growing up. I had done a lot of commercials where there's wasn't a lot of speaking and I'm always sort of reacting to the voice-over or the announcer or something. And I could mimic well, too. And so with a difficult role, if I was having a problem in something, Bob could guide me as to the best way to do it. And I seemed pretty perceptive and able to mimic well. So I think that combination, and of course, he said there was some magic there as well. I don't know.

BOB CLARK: Yeah, he was a pro. And he would want me to act the scenes out for him. And it was damned embarrassing because I would act them out and then he would turn around and do subtle nuances I hadn't begun to put into it as little-boy stuff. So I said, "Peter, do you want me to go on doing this?" He says, "Yeah." I just didn't know what I could forget about, you know, where I'm going to go. Where I'm going to move and I could just kind of be the guy. So we worked that way, but believe me, his force was so much better than mine it was absurd. I took him always through narration. I did the narration off camera. He needed it and this was meticulous timing. This wasn't just thrown together. It was very, very carefully thought-out. Meticulous and we didn't vary from Jean, from our script narration very much at all. So his—[it] is very difficult to fill those moments and be alive while the camera's on him and telling you what he's doing. And some people felt, well, that's quite a redundant technique. That's not true. I think it's wonderful to hear a man in his forties reflecting on what he thinks he did when he was nine years old, and we're seeing what he really did and that. [There were] often contradictions between what Jean Shepherd is saying he's doing and what the boy's actually doing. I think that's part of the depth of the work.

JEAN SHEPHERD: Every day we would have a plan of what we're going to shoot. The night before Bob and I would go out to dinner or something with Lee. You got to remember Lee's involved in this, and we'd sit down and really discuss what worked on our shoot today and how it's going to be shot. Give you an example of that, how the father and his wife [Melinda Dillon] were not getting along. They didn't get along together at all. And I wanted to make sure that that was brought out, that they weren't kidding around. Most people who see the movie really don't get that because it's done very subtly. So we would work together before the day and then go off and do it. That's all there is to that.

PETER BILLINGSLEY: I'd done a lot of films prior to this, and there's always speculation on the set of, oh, you'll be a star after this. This one will be so wonderful. The different thing about *Christmas Story* was it seemed like everybody had something invested in it. And you didn't really know why. It wasn't talked about it. There was no hype about it. Everybody just seemed so focused. And I think I picked up on that, and I picked up on the passion of Jean and the passion of Bob and of Darren and everybody involved in the film. And we all kind of got into a rhythm, which I've never been involved with since. And it seems like we all do so many of these things, and once in a great while you get magic. And you don't really know why. It was a wonderful story, it was a great group of people, and the timing was right, and, yeah, everybody did have a lot invested in it. And it was a tremendously tough shooting schedule. We were isolated in Cleveland and Canada, and I think it was like one big family, sort of. We were all away from our homes for a long time. We were working grueling hours. We were working often from 6 PM to 6 AM, and everybody was quite focused. And for all of those reasons, we got some great movie magic.

Melinda Dillon as Ralphie's mother in *A Christmas Story*.

Darren McGavin:

PETER BILLINGSLEY: I had never met anybody who knew so much about the entire process. And I distinctly remember Darren on numerous occasions, when there would be a problem. It could have been something with the grips or with the lighting, and Darren would have the answer to the problem, and immediately. It could be something so simple as a lighting thing. A couple of tech guys would be talking it over. Darren would be sitting on the couch waiting for them, and he'd just holler out, "Why don't you scrim it with a wedge over on the right side?" And they'd kind of look at him blankly and say, "He's right." Darren is very hands-on, and he's very involved in the entire process. I wasn't necessarily intimidated, but I certainly kept my ears open around him.

BOB CLARK: Darren knows this. Of course we went through a long list of guys before we got to Darren. Jack Nicholson at one time. I pitched two things to Jack, that being one. I think he actually wanted to do that one, but the studio wanted him to do the other one. So I don't think they ever took it seriously that he might do *Christmas Story*. I had a long list of people, and near the end I always had Darren in the back of my mind, you know. They were looking to get bigger stars. He got it overnight. He loved it, and it was the beginning of a friendship that's been going on for fifteen years now. And four or five movies together.

JEAN SHEPHERD: Well, Darren's another story. I like Darren. Darren's a good man. And I take credit for casting him in that. When we were first debating as to who was going to play these roles, I was talking to Bob, and I said I would like to have, if at all possible, Darren McGavin. Because Darren did a series on TV called *The Night Stalker*. It was a wonderful series. He played a Chicago reporter who is always racing around town in his little Mustang with the little hat on his head trying to track down everything from Godzilla to...it was all about ghosts and all that stuff. And so I thought he was just right. You know, he had that certain smart-ass quality about him that I saw in this character, the father. This was not a conventional father, you know. And you couldn't get a conventional actor to play that, who will play it like a father. In fact, I wanted an actor who hated kids. And that's what he did. He really did.

DARREN MCGAVIN: Well, we had not met before that. We hadn't had any relationships at all. The casting of me in the role was really at Jean's behest. He wanted somebody like me, so they called me and I said, let me read the script and sure I'll do it. We got along famously together, Bob and I. Well, we hadn't met before this initial relationship that we established on *A Christmas Story*. And we, as in all relationships in creativity, we kind of boxed around with each other to find out what were the extent of his parameters and mine. And we found they fit very well together. He was very open to change and interpretation. And he served as much as an audience as anything else really.

BOB CLARK: Darren's very strong minded, but also wants to know. He listens. He came with only–like a few days rehearsals is all he had. He said, "I want [to] start expansive." The character is expansive. The old man is expansive. So there was no need for the actor to be. Darren's a splendid actor, so he immediately went into his lower resources and his most overtly real person, but then he had to be big the way the old man's big. And I think he's brilliant.

Melinda Dillon:

PETER BILLINGSLEY: Melinda Dillon was so loving, and she really almost filled the void of my mom, who was traveling a bit at the time. I had my brother to come up and be with me on the set, and my grandmother was on the set at times. And when somebody wasn't around, she would really step in and fill a very nice void both on and off the set.

JEAN SHEPHERD: She's kind of—at least as far as I was concerned—kind of an enigma. She didn't mix much with me or other people who were involved in the movie. She'd come and go. She'd come and do her scenes and leave, but with not much socializing. She seems to be a perfectly nice woman, I don't know.

BOB CLARK: Melinda was coming off of *Close Encounters of the Third Kind*, and she seemed to be perfect. She had a quintessential Midwestern feel to me. I think she is from the Midwest actually. We met once and we had great rapport, and it was a great cast. It was one of those movies where it was joyous all the time. It was never any discomfort. Anything but pleasure. Our little boy, Ian Petrella, who played Randy, the younger brother—I didn't get him until two days after we started shooting. We were already filming and they flew him up to my house.

JEAN SHEPHERD: I think the best scene that she did was when the little brother, Randy, was hiding under the sink. Do you remember that? Well, he was hiding because he was afraid that his brother was in trouble, and the father is going to come home and really give him hell. So he's scared. He's sitting under the sink hiding. And she opens the door, and there he is sitting there looking scared. And she says to Randy, she says, "Daddy is not going to kill Ralphie. Now would you like a glass of milk?" And he sort of moves his head a little bit like, yeah. So she gives him the milk and then closes the door. Leaves him in there. It was a great moment. It really was.

The Production:

JEAN SHEPHERD: The interiors were shot in Toronto for a number of reasons. The Canadian government put some money in the movie. The exteriors were shot in Cleveland, which was exactly right for what I saw the movie to be. It was a story about a kid that was growing up in a tough steel mill town. You might say total industrial background. Most novels and movies are written about kids that grew up in a New York apartment or in LA or something. I don't know of any other movie, really, about a kid growing up in the shadow of the blast furnace.

DARREN MCGAVIN: We shot it in Cleveland. All the exteriors and the house and all the backyard and the trees and winter, but we had a huge problem because there was no snow that winter. So when we moved up to Toronto to shoot interiors, we still had a lot of the exteriors to do. And we finally had to go out to parking lots where it [had] snowed two or three weeks before and pick up all the snow that had been shoved off to one side and put it in a truck and dump it and put it in the alley. It was difficult, touch and go there for a while.

PETER BILLINGSLEY: Well, certainly to shoot, my favorite scene was when we were in Higbee's department store and visiting Santa, because they had built this big slide for us. And so in between takes, during lunch, during dinner breaks, we were constantly sliding down this thing and trying to invent new ways to get down, much to the horror of Bob and Jean because they were afraid we were going to break our necks. And seemingly the whole process was fun. Everyone was able to create an environment, especially for myself and for Ian, who played my brother in the film—we were pretty young guys and thrown into a situation where there was a tremendous amount of work expected. Everybody seemingly joined and tried to help as much as possible.

JEAN SHEPHERD: That was a good scene. As far as I'm concerned, that was the cinematic highlight of the movie. That scene with Santa Claus and climbing up the mountain. See, that's almost word for word from the book, that scene. And it worked beautifully. He got up to the top, and when he asked for a BB gun, Santa Claus looked at him and said, "You'll shoot your eye out, kid." And Santa just leaned back and took his big rubber boot and he just went whop. He pushed him down the chute, and that was the scene. Peter did it so well, he had a scared look on his face, but at the same time, he had a look that says, "I'm going to tell this guy what I want. I don't care what he says." And that way—I think that scene has gotten more public reaction than any other single scene in the movie.

PETER BILLINGSLEY: I think probably the most difficult scene to shoot was when I finally got the gun and I went outside on the back porch and I lined up the target and aimed the gun and shot myself in the eye. That was one of the coldest days, and I was in very thin pj's and nothing underneath and was laying in snow. We had a house at the time, which was sort of a gutted house we weren't shooting in, but [it] was the exterior. And so they just had these little mini space heaters in there, and so I remember we'd do a take and then I'd run inside and sort of try to pry my fingers open in front of the space heater. That was probably the most grueling shoot. Actually, all that stuff in downtown Cleveland we shot at night from about 6 PM to 6 AM. And they were shutting down the downtown square and they would light up Higbee's, and they would dress it with all the street cars and the people. That was a pretty grueling shoot at times.

JEAN SHEPHERD: One of the most memorable things about the production is how damn cold it was. Jesus. I mean talk about freezing your keister, it was real. When those kids went out walking along the street in that snow and all that, the kid was freezing in his little suit, that little snow suit. It was so cold they really, really weren't acting any more. They were crying and yelling. And it just fit when the kid [Scott Schwartz] went out and put his tongue on the pole, that steel light pole out in front of the school. And when he started to cry, he was crying. That kid was genuinely crying. And his tongue was stuck on that damn light pole. And all the kids ran away, but when they took him off the pole, he was crying. They brought him into the school. That's where we were shooting. And he was crying, and if you want to have memories of this thing, there was a lot of realism in this movie that wasn't just written in. It was there.

Ralphie (Peter Billingsley) tells Santa his fondest wish—to own a Genuine Carbine Air Rifle—in *A Christmas Story*.

PETER BILLINGSLEY: Obviously, as a kid actor, you work with kids a lot. I think what works is that you let kids be kids as much as possible when you're not shooting. And Scott [Schwartz] and myself and Ian and R. D. [Robb] got along great and we were palling around constantly. After work we'd terrorize the hotels we were staying in, and on the weekends we'd try to find fun things to do. Again, Bob knew when to step back and when we were being overworked and just said, "All right, guys, have fun for a few minutes and then let's get back to work." It was a great environment to play in, because we were outside in Toronto and there was snow on the ground, which is an instant recipe for fun with kids.

Lost Scenes:

PETER BILLINGSLEY: There were a couple of extra fantasy scenes; Ralphie was constantly dreaming. There was one in particular that I remember which was a Flash Gordon sequence where I had my gun and was dressed in these very skimpy silver shorts and this odd hat. It was set in the year 3000, and I was with Flash Gordon and we were shooting what I believe was a dragon. He was having a hard time with his weapon, and I was able to come in with my Red Ryder BB gun and take it out. I think when they tested the film, people liked the fantasy sequences and dream sequences, but they liked so much what was going on with the family that [Bob Clark] chose to cut that scene out.

The Bumpus Hounds:

DARREN MCGAVIN: The turkey scene. Yeah, well, we had the dogs, the pack of hounds that were next-door. And I think they starved them to death because we had the scene with the turkey on the table, ready to be sliced for dinner, and of course, somebody opened the front door and here they came. And they headed right for the thing. They took it off the table. They started fighting in the kitchen set and out the backdoor and we picked it up, of course, again in the exterior. And they didn't stop. I mean they had a great turkey dinner.

JEAN SHEPHERD: Those bloodhounds. Oh, they were crazy. We were in Cleveland, and we got in touch with a company that had dogs. And they said, "Oh, we've got some dogs, but they're not trained. They're not movie dogs–so watch out, all right?" And so he arrived in this big station wagon with a whole crowd of these things. Oh, I don't know, there must have been ten of them. And they're all big and smelly. And pushing and shoving and yapping and hollering, and they let them out of the truck and they ran around the set. And they're sniffing at everybody and yelping. And Darren liked them right away. He liked those dogs. He said, "Oh boy, these are real dogs. These are real dogs. They're not movie dogs. Look at that dog over there. He's peeing on something." It was a riot from the minute those dogs arrived.

They were as untrained as a dog can get. And a dog doesn't take much training. You offer a nice fresh roast turkey, he'll go after it. And all these dogs were big dogs. They were all hungry. And they went after that turkey and they were yelling and rolling on the floor just like you saw in the movie. Yapping and hollering. Darren ran out. He's supposed to stop them. Well, there was no way he could stop them. And he's saying "Get out of here. Get out of here, you bums." One of the dogs turned and growled, gave him a bad look. And he ran back out of the kitchen, and the minute he was gone, this big daddy dog grabbed the turkey and ran out of the backyard into the snow. And that was the last we saw of that turkey. But boy, what a moment that was. It was a great moment. One take. You know, when the turkey's been eaten by a bunch of dogs, you're not saying let's go from the top and do it again.

Ralphie (Peter Billingsley) imagines he is saving his family from danger in *A Christmas Story*.

Tough Times and Success:

JEAN SHEPHERD: We never thought, "Gee, we're making a classic." And we just thought we would make a very good movie and it would be funny. It wasn't originally accepted, you know. M-G-M wasn't going to release it. They didn't like it. They released it with great reluctance. And when they released it, all of a sudden the people started to talk about it. They didn't put any advertising in it, very little. We were a little disappointed at that, and we realized that it was because the studio didn't believe in the movie. And they weren't going to go out on a limb. They're just going to put that out on the marketplace and that's it. Walk away. Because their big movie at the time was *Yentl*. Remember that? A turkey of the first order. We went out and–I remember Lee and I were coming back. We have a house in Maine and it was late fall and we were driving back. We stopped at a hamburger joint and I went out and, while I was going out, I saw there was a newsstand there. And I bought a paper. And by God, on the front page of *USA Today* was a big picture. It says, "Sleeper Movie Sweeps the Nation" or something of that nature. I couldn't believe it. I took the paper back to Lee and I threw it in the car and said, "Lee, what do you think of this?" She says, "Oh, my God. That's unbelievable." So M-G-M wasn't prepared for [it], nor was anybody else– including me and Lee and even Bob, I suppose–but by God, it really went off, went off right into the stratosphere. Hasn't stopped since. That's really surprising. I think that's the most surprising thing about this whole movie issue: what an unexpected success it was. And today, it's far more popular than it was when it first came out. Because now people talk about it. They know about the movie. But in those days, it was just a little tiny few who would sit in the theater, huddled together laughing at the kid with his tongue on the lamppost.

BOB CLARK: *A Christmas Story* was very lucky to make it to the screen at all. Freddie Fields started the movie, and his administration left and was to be replaced. And for an interim period of three or four months, the powers that be, the head of distribution, whoever they were, said this movie didn't test well, because it didn't. Tested okay, but not particularly. And if kids want to see it, adults will not be interested in this movie, so we're not going to release it. Frank Yablans came in to take over the studio, and I asked for a meeting. And Frank said, "Tell me what you think and I'll look at the movie." I told him what I thought, and he looked at the movie and called back and says, "They're wrong, you're right. This movie has a chance. We're going to give it a crack." And we had like three weeks to open it at Thanksgiving. We opened the week before Thanksgiving and did very well. I think we did like—I can't remember, averaged about $4,000 per theater. We did about $2.8 million in 800 theaters. The second week the movie went double. It's the only movie ever to go up 100 percent. It went up to like $8,000 per theater. But the irony was that we had booked it so late that we only had a four-week run. We went out of the theaters on December 16. So *Christmas Story* did not play about a hundred theaters. It didn't play over Christmas. It went out of the theaters averaging over $3,500 per screen, which today would be more like $7,000. Can you imagine a movie going out of the theaters today averaging $7,000 per theater? So we did about $20 million box office in the three and a half weeks it had in 800 theaters. So it actually did pretty well, but it never got back. After Christmas they tried to put it back in, but it's called *A Christmas Story*. It's a bit of a myth that it didn't do well—it did pretty well considering. It was the number-one movie for two weeks. And like I said, it was the only movie ever to double its box office from week one to week two. But, that was its history.

Darren McGavin in *A Christmas Story*.

Why We Love A Christmas Story:

DARREN MCGAVIN: Well, I think it strikes a chord in all of America. I think everybody who has a familial relationship with an old man and with their mother who's always trying to fix things up and make things work. And the old man doesn't give a damn, you know. And I think that strikes a chord of congeniality really with American people.

PETER BILLINGSLEY: I certainly didn't identify with the specifics at the time, but what I think makes the film great is that the character is a universal boy. And whether it's a gun or whether it's a train set, everybody can identify with that one thing, as a boy, we've longed for so much. And I think all of the obstacles that he perceived and that he faced along the way, we can all identify with as young boys or even as girls....Jean had seemed to create something, which he's done so many times, which is a character and really a family unit that had problems and concerns and loves that are similar to the family units that we all want to be or that we can relate to. And it was a very easy fit into that mold. So I don't think it was only my character. It was the brother. It was the parents. It was the neighbors. It was really the whole world that he created which was a very rare world to step into.

BOB CLARK: I am unabashedly fond of it. I remember a review saying in effect, "So you think this is a sweet little Christmas movie, where Santa comes but let me tell you a few things." He goes on to list the mom's lying to dad, dad's lying to mom, the kid's lying to everybody. Santa kicks the kid in the face. But it's still touching and enormously affecting despite the fact that it's a tougher movie. I'm very gratified people do love *A Christmas Story*. When they do like it, they like it profoundly. It's very deep with some people. I was sitting with my ex-wife and my kids in a restaurant in New Hampshire, and over the booth behind us, we heard people talking. We knew it was lines from *Christmas Story*. And they proceeded over the entire course of our dinner, this family, the mother, father, two boys, acted out the whole movie. Did the whole ninety-five minutes worth of dialogue in the movie over dinner. I was flabbergasted. There are people who know all the movies. It's not uncommon. But a family acting out the movie—my wife wanted me to go introduce myself. But that would have been...they couldn't have believed it.

Gremlins (1984)

Co-star Hoyt Axton once described Joe Dante's *Gremlins* as "*E. T.* with teeth." There are certainly similarities: Both films feature strange and adorable otherworldly creatures, and both teeter between sweetness and horror. There are homages, too: Steven Spielberg, director of *E.T.* and executive producer of *Gremlins*, makes a cameo appearance when Hoyt Axton's crackpot inventor attends an inventors' convention. And when a terrorized woman tries to make a phone call, her telephone cord is snapped by a spindly hand as we hear a gremlin croak, "Phone home..."

Gremlins is, in short, as much a movie about other movies as it is about tiny, gleefully malicious monsters that overtake a small, picture-perfect town on Christmas Eve. It's chock full of classic movie clips—characters watch *It's a Wonderful Life*, *Invasion of the Body Snatchers* (1956), and *To Please a Lady* (1950) on television; and the gremlins all congregate in the local movie house to enjoy—and they do enjoy it!—*Snow White and the Seven Dwarfs* (1937). There are even oblique movie references: a movie theater marquee advertises *A Boy's Life* and *Watch the Skies*—the respective working titles for *E.T.* and *Close Encounters of the Third Kind*.

But perhaps the slyest movie in-joke is that director Joe Dante has created a snow-covered town, Kingston Falls, of such Christmasy perfection that it could only exist in a

Great Christmas TV

✳   ✳   ✳

*C*hristmas is television's favorite holiday. If a TV series makes it through an entire season, its creators will probably come up with at least one Christmas episode–a takeoff on *A Christmas Carol*, for instance, or a ponderous sermon on The Real Meaning of Christmas. And more television specials are undoubtedly devoted to Christmas than to any other single subject.

Most of these seasonal shows, because of the very nature of television, are disposable entertainments. But a few–a very few–have become enduring classics in their own right and are as welcome on the holiday viewing menu as any of the great Christmas movies.

Two animated specials from the sixties have joined that elite company of TV Christmas classics: "A Charlie Brown Christmas," based on Charles Schultz's "Peanuts" characters, and that inspired collaboration between animation great Chuck Jones and children's book legend Theodore Geisel–"Dr. Seuss' How the Grinch Stole Christmas!"

"A Charlie Brown Christmas" finds its sad-sack main character in a quandary. He wants to find the real meaning of Christmas, while all around him his friends are only interested in presents, parties, and other trappings of a commercial holiday (his bossy friend Lucy is incensed because she never gets what she wants: "Real estate!"). Along the way, Charlie Brown adopts a pathetic little Christmas tree and learns what Christmas is all about from Linus, who recites the story of the Nativity from the Gospel of St. Luke. All the kids join in helping to decorate Charlie Brown's tree and end by singing "Hark the Heralds Angels Sing" as the snow begins to fall.

Rather crudely animated and decidedly low-key in its humor, "A Charlie Brown Christmas" easily achieved number-one rating when it first aired on December 9, 1965. In fact, it continued to win its time slot every time it was repeated for years. In addition, it won the Peabody Award for Broadcasting Excellence. It still airs every Christmas and remains as popular as ever, one of the few Christmas specials with an overtly religious theme to have achieved that kind of popularity.

Chuck Jones and Theodore Geisel's "How the Grinch Stole Christmas!" is about the Grinch, a grouchy creature who lives on a mountain above Whoville. The Grinch hates the gentle Whos who live there, and especially hates the idea of Christmas. Why? Well, it might be because his shoes are too tight, or it might be because his heart is two sizes too small. Either way, he determines to wreck the holiday for all the Whos. Breaking into their houses, he steals their trees, presents, and decorations and prepares to cast all the bounty into the abyss. But as Christmas morning dawns, he find that the Whos are happily celebrating Christmas, even without all the trappings and presents. Now, the Grinch's heart grows three sizes larger as he realizes that the meaning of Christmas doesn't come from gifts and greed, but from togetherness, generosity, and faith.

Chuck Jones—the animation genius who worked with such stars as Bugs Bunny, Daffy Duck, and Elmer Fudd, and who created the Road Runner and Wile E. Coyote—based his character design directly on Geisel's distinctive original art. "How the Grinch Stole Christmas!" looks very much like the Dr. Seuss book come to life, but with a definite patina of Jones. The contemplative blink, the limber movement, the droopy ears and soulful eyes of the Grinch's perpetually apprehensive dog Max, all come from Jones, while the spirit of the enterprise is Dr. Seuss's to the tiniest detail. "How the Grinch Stole Christmas!" is a perfect collaboration, an admirable melding of styles.

Unlike "A Charlie Brown Christmas," "How the Grinch Stole Christmas!" is superbly animated with all the energy and fluidity of one of Jones's Warner Bros. cartoons. It first aired on December 18, 1966. While it was never quite the runaway hit that the former cartoon was, it remains among the most memorable of Christmas TV shows, and the Grinch himself has joined the elite company of great Christmas characters like Ebenezer Scrooge and Tiny Tim.

The hilarious and borderline-surreal "Pee-wee's Playhouse Christmas Special" from 1988 almost qualifies as an animated show because its main character, Pee-wee Herman (Paul Reubens) is as close to a cartoon character as a human can get. Filled with bizarre guest stars–Zsa Zsa Gabor, the Del Rubio Triplets, Charo, Grace Jones (singing a weird rendition of "The Little Drummer Boy"), and others–"Pee-wee's Playhouse Christmas Special" is a wonderful mixture of innocence and sophistication, with delightfully oddball jokes such as when Pee-wee gives his friend Miss Yvonne (Lynne Stewart) a bottle of perfume–"Eau de Pee-wee." She sniffs and says approvingly, "It smells just like you!"

"Pee-wee's Playhouse Christmas Special" is available on video, but several truly memorable Christmas episodes are not. The brilliant Canadian series *SCTV* offered Christmas-themed shows in both 1981 and 1982. The first centered around a cast party at the fictional TV station at which the show's various characters–all portrayed by the seven members of the *SCTV* troupe–interact. One subplot featured drunken TV host Johnny LaRue's (John Candy) quest for an expensive crane to shoot his next TV movie. When the station boss Guy Caballero (Joe Flaherty) cruelly sends him out into the freezing night to do an episode of "Street Beef," a man-on-the-street show, LaRue drinks himself into a stupor after being deserted by his cameraman. LaRue wakes up with a bright light shining in his eyes and finds that Santa Claus himself has brought him a huge crane, festooned with Christmas lights.

As the next season's Christmas episode begins, the crane is being repossessed to take care of LaRue's gambling debts. He determines to go back into the street, wait for Santa, and ask for another. But what he finds is something else instead.

The pair of *SCTV* Christmas shows are alternately hilarious, strange, and touching. Johnny LaRue's quest for Santa is the spine (and heart) of the show, but there are other remarkable bits. The most memorable, perhaps, is "Ed Grimley in 'The Fella Who Couldn't Wait For Christmas,'" in which the pointy-haired Grimley (Martin Short) paces his room frantically waiting for sunup, imagining the wonderful Christmas morning that just won't come. And there's a Christmas visit with the polka-playing Schmenge brothers (John Candy and Eugene Levy) who explain the quaint customs of their native Leutonia ("where trees are now extinct").

Some of the *SCTV* crew later worked on a Canadian comedy series called *Maniac Mansion*, and produced a superlative Christmas episode there. *Maniac Mansion* is about a crackpot inventor, Fred Edison (Joe Flaherty), whose house is set on a meteor and whose botched experiments have left him with a four-year-old son, Turner (George Buza), who is over six feet tall and weighs in at about 300 pounds, and a brother-in-law, Harry (John Hemphill), who is part human, part fly. Edison also lives with his wife (Deborah Theaker), their two relatively normal children, Ike (Avi Phillips) and Tina (Kathleen Robertson), and Harry's wife (Mary Charlotte Wilcox).

In the Christmas episode, "Good Cheer on Ya!", a cruel neighbor kid has told Turner that there is no Santa, and even if there were, he'd never believe Turner was only four. Meanwhile Harry's relentlessly cheery–and relatively stupid–twin brother (Hemphill) is making his way to the Edison's from Canada, first by dogsled, then by clinging to the tire of an airplane. The family is concerned about uncle Eddie being lost in the storm, and Turner prays that he will give up all his toys if only his uncle can get home safely. Santa hears his prayer and comes to get Turner so the two of them can rescue Eddie.

This oddball show was always notable for its ability to skate between crazy moments of hilarity and true family warmth. "Good Cheer on Ya!" is a superior example of how well both attitudes could exist within the same frame.

There are many great TV Christmas shows–"A Christmas Story," a 1960 episode of *The Andy Griffith Show*; a magical foray into the supernatural in the teen-angst drama *My So-Called Life*; a hilariously stupid episode of *Dragnet* revolving around a stolen Baby Jesus from a Nativity scene. Many of the best are recycled endlessly every Christmas. But others require a little detective work to be found. Some of the best of them are worth the trouble; they offer moments that are as funny, as moving, and as memorable as anything in any Great Christmas Movie.

movie. And he has peopled it with an impressive roster of great character actors, which any movie buff worth his salted popcorn will recognize on sight: Roger Corman regular Dick Miller, Ken Tobey (star of *The Thing*), William Schallert, Harry Carey Jr., Jackie Joseph (the loopy girlfriend from the original *Little Shop of Horrors*), and Charlie Chan's number-one son, Keye Luke. Dante even brought in animation legend Chuck Jones for a brief cameo in a bar—just one of many tributes the director has paid to Jones over the years. (In *Explorers* from 1985, for instance, the kids go to Charles M. Jones High School.) Also popping up briefly at the inventors' fair, along with Spielberg (with a broken leg), are *Gremlins*' composer Jerry Goldsmith, Robbie the Robot from *Forbidden Planet* (1955), and the original Time Machine from George Pal's 1960 film (it's only there for one shot, though; seconds later it's gone).

"The movie is its own triple bill," Dante said. "It's a remake of my other movies and a remake of every movie alluded to in it. I like movies. And I like to make movies for people who like movies."

The birth of *Gremlins* came when screenwriter Chris Columbus was twenty-one years old, attending New York University Film School and living in a loft in the garment district that was alive with creepy, crawly things. He said in 1984, "When I went to sleep at night, I could hear mice scurrying along the floor. I slept with my arm draped over the side of the bed, hanging just above floor level, and I kept having this nightmare of waking up with a mouse nibbling my fingers. That's how I got the idea for *Gremlins*."

Gremlins inspired a certain amount of controversy upon its original release because its cute, cuddly main character, Gizmo was so alluring to kids—and was energetically marketed as such, with Gizmo dolls and other kinds of *Gremlins*-related toys. But the extreme, sometimes sickening (but almost always hilarious) violence of the film was definitely not suited for kids.

Gremlins opens on Christmas Eve in some anonymous city's Chinatown. Inventor Rand Peltzer (Axton) visits a basement shop hoping to sell his latest invention, the Bathroom Buddy, a contraption with every imaginable toiletry item attached, to the owner (Keye Luke), and also hoping to buy an unusual Christmas present for his son Billy (Zach Galligan). He finds a strange little furry creature called a Mogwai, with big lovable eyes, huge ears, and a beguiling singing voice. Rand buys the creature from the store owner's grandson—against the wishes of the grandfather—and is given three strict warnings: keep the Mogwai out of bright light, which can kill him; never let him get near water; and never, no matter how much he begs, never feed him after midnight.

Of course, it's only a matter of time until each of these rules has been broken. When water accidentally spills on the Mogwai—whom Rand has named Gizmo—he reproduces five more furry little creatures. Only these aren't cute; they're crazy and malicious. Pretty soon, they've multiplied into hundreds of gremlins, each one set on destruction—and fun. They're mean-natured, spiteful, and rambunctious, and laugh maniacally as they wreak havoc; the gremlins are less like conventional movie monsters, more like sadistic frat boys on spring break.

Phoebe Cates, Zach Galligan, and Gizmo in *Gremlins*.

The Christmas atmosphere of the film is perfect, from the beautiful decorations to the more whimsical touches—such as the young son (Corey Feldman) of a Christmas tree lot owner, who is forced, to his disgust, to dress like a tree himself. But Christmas also sets the scene for some of *Gremlins'* darkest bits of humor. Billy's girlfriend, Kate (Phoebe Cates), hates Christmas but won't tell him why. Finally, she tells him about the Christmas when she was nine. Her father never came home from work, and she and her mother were frantic with worry. After several days, they gave him up for lost. One night, she went to light a fire, "and that's when I noticed the smell." Turns out her father had dressed as Santa and was coming down the chimney with gifts, but he broke his neck on the way down and was stuck there all that time. "And that," Kate says, "is how I found out there's no Santa Claus."

Kingston Falls is slightly terrorized by one filthy-rich Mrs. Deagle (Polly Holliday), a combination of Ebenezer Scrooge and the Wicked Witch of the West. She verbally assaults an out-of-work mother who can't pay her rent and calls her two children "deadbeats." When Billy's dog destroys one of her Christmas ornaments, Mrs. Deagle doesn't want to be reimbursed for the damages—she wants the dog to die for it, just like Miss Gulch in *The Wizard of*

Four gremlins spread Christmas cheer in the movie *Gremlins*.

Oz. She even paraphrases that memorable meany when she says to the dog, "I'll get you—when you least expect it!"

When the gremlins inevitably get to Mrs. Deagle's house, there are two in-jokes waiting for them, one obvious, the other less so: Scattered here and there are numerous portraits of the late Mr. Deagle—the great actor of the thirties and forties, Edward Arnold. The more obscure, and therefore more satisfying, joke is that Mrs. Deagle, on this Christmas Eve, has obviously expected a Scrooge-like redemption. When she fears that she's about to be killed in a particularly imaginative way by the gremlins, she keeps muttering to herself, "I'm not ready! I'm not ready!" It's as though old Ebenezer had been run over by a carriage on his way home from work on Christmas Eve—no happy ending.

But, as Steven Spielberg said when it was pointed out to him that no one dies in his science fiction or horror movies, *E.T., Close Encounters,* and *Poltergeist* (produced by Spielberg and directed by Tobe Hooper), "I'm not sure if anybody really dies in this one either. I never saw the gremlins as homicidal, psychotic, maniacal killers. Perhaps they are the dark side of the founding father of creatures great and small: They're Walt Disney's id." Indeed, the couple played by Dick Miller and Jackie Joseph appear to meet their maker in *Gremlins* but show up hale and hearty in *Gremlins 2: The New Batch* (1990), a sequel that is even wilder and funnier than the original—but it has no Christmas connection, so that is all the notice we will take of it here.

Most of the violence in *Gremlins* is so comically over the top that it probably disturbed very few children, no matter how many parents were concerned about it. The most notable gross-out moments come when they attack Billy's mother (Frances McCain) in her kitchen. She's a match for them, though—she traps one in the blender and purees him, hacks another to pieces with a butcher knife, and traps a third in the microwave where he explodes in a goopy mess of glop.

According to Dante, all of the mockery and sick humor of the film was grafted by him and screenwriter Chris Columbus onto an original story that was supposed to play out as straight horror. "It was more of a horror film when we started," he told an interviewer. "The gremlins didn't do anything funny; they did *terrible* things. It was something that had just been done a lot. The trick was to do something different. It isn't worth doing unless it can be its own self. So, as we started to embellish it, the picture started to take on a somewhat warmer quality. We soft-pedaled even what little violence we had actually photographed, but not so much that we would take the edge off. I was afraid that without the edge, it'd become a picture that doesn't get to be what it's supposed to be."

The gremlins themselves were designed by Chris Walas, who had worked with Dante on his horror send-up *Piranha* (1978) and on Spielberg's *Raiders of the Lost Ark* (1981). "Every shot required different gremlins," Walas said at the time. "We created twelve versions of Gizmo and fourteen Stripes (the main bad gremlin), each used in a different closeup or for a specific movement or to express a new emotion. One gremlin had to be able to inhale and exhale cigarette smoke, another had to throw dishes at Billy's mother, and another had to ride its skateboard through the department store. With all the rewriting of the script during production, we were making puppets until the last days of shooting."

Gremlins is a maliciously funny and improbably lovable Christmas present of a movie. There's a laugh for every scream, a joke for every plot twist, and more movie references than you can count. It's never quite warm, and there isn't an ounce of sentiment—remember Kate's dad stuck in that chimney. But it rewards annual holiday viewings just the same—*Gremlins* is the warped, hilarious underside to *It's a Wonderful Life*.

Mary Steenburgen stars as
Ginnie Grainger in *One Magic
Christmas*.

Ginnie (Mary Steenburgen)
stands beside her family (*left to
right*: Arthur Hill, Elizabeth
Harnois, Robbie Magwood, and
Gary Basaraba).

One Magic Christmas (1985)

AS MENTIONED EARLIER, Christmas movies often have a
dark side: Consider George Bailey's awful day that nearly
ends with his suicide in *It's a Wonderful Life*. But there
are few that are as relentlessly bleak and heart-wrenching
as Phillip Borsos's *One Magic Christmas*. Although the
film ends in a moment as warm and beautiful as any
Christmas movie has ever given us, the road to that
moment is rough going indeed, filled with one disturbing
instance after another of loss, death, grief, and despair.

As *One Magic Christmas* opens, things are not going
well for the Grainger family at Christmas. Jack (Gary
Basaraba) has been out of work since June. His wife,
Ginnie (Mary Steenbergen), is working grueling hours for
minimum wage at the checkout counter at the local gro-
cery store, barely earning enough to keep her family
together. Their company-owned house is about to be
rented out from under them, and it looks like Santa will be
bypassing the Grainger home, to the dismay of nine-year-
old Cal (Robbie Magwood) and six-year-old Abbie
(Elisabeth Harnois). "I don't think Santa Claus is coming
this year," says Cal, "because we're too poor." Abbie
responds, "No, it's because I didn't write a letter to
Santa."

The Graingers have only $5,000 in the bank, which
Ginnie wants to save against the future. Jack wants to give
his kids a good Christmas—and he also dreams of opening
his own bicycle shop, an enterprise that will take precisely
$5,000 to get started.

Help arrives in the figure of Gideon (Harry Dean
Stanton), a Christmas angel who still dresses like the
cowboy he once was. It's Gideon's job to help one person
every year get into the Christmas spirit. He introduces
himself to Abbie when she comes out to mail her letter to
Santa, and he promises that this year Ginnie is the one
he's going to help. Gideon gives back to Abbie her letter
to Santa and instructs her to have her mother mail it.

Gideon, however, is not like the angel Dudley in *The
Bishop's Wife* (1947), who helps his charges through
gentle persuasion and unobtrusive magic tricks. Gideon
helps Ginnie find her Christmas spirit by systematically—
one might say cruelly—taking away everything she has:
her husband is killed in a bank robbery, her children are
kidnapped by the robber, and they apparently die when he

plunges the getaway car off a bridge and into a freezing river. Ginnie at this point *wishes* that she could have a day as good as George Bailey's.

But just when *One Magic Christmas* gets to its bleakest moment, it starts to justify its title with moments of sheer magic. The children are rescued from the river by Gideon. And when Abbie asks Gideon to bring her father back to life, too, he says that he can't do something like that–but that maybe Santa Claus can. Together, they go to the North Pole where Abbie meets one of movies' best Santas (Jan Rubes)–a stern but gentle man with a wild, unkempt beard. He explains to the little girl that he can't bring her father back to life, but that her mother can. He doesn't, however, explain exactly how this can happen.

Ginnie bids good night to Abbie.

Santa takes Abbie through his workshop–peopled not with elves but with ordinary humans of different nationalities and dressed in clothing from different periods. They have come to the North Pole after death to spend a happy eternity making toys. In his files, Santa finds a letter Ginnie wrote him when she was eight; he gives it to Abbie and tells her to give it to her mother.

The letter does indeed help Ginnie regain her Christmas spirit, and she finally mails Abbie's letter, an act that breaks the spell and gives her a second chance at the day where everything went wrong.

Like Ebenezer Scrooge, Ginnie Grainger is changed by a vision. She hasn't been cruel or miserly, just too weighed down by the oppressiveness of life, too concerned about daily problems to allow a little magic into her life. "You'd be better off if you believed in Santa, like Abbie," her husband tells her. And she replies, "Like you, you mean." Jack does indeed believe in the nature of Santa, the idea that little acts of generosity–and, occasionally, silliness– are essential ingredients to life. The magic in this *Magic Christmas* comes when Ginnie finds that childlike faith that she has long since lost. She avoids the tragic incidents of that Christmas Eve, not by any elaborate plan to make sure that her husband and kids don't show up at the bank, but by a simple gesture of kindness and humanity to the man whose desperation would otherwise lead him to commit the crime. As terrible and terrifying as the process was, Ginnie's happy ending comes with a profound message. Her deliverance has not come from a miracle but through the realization that the cliches of

Harry Dean Stanton stars as the Christmas angel Gideon in *One Magic Christmas*.

Elizabeth Harnois stars as Abbie Grainger in *One Magic Christmas*.

Christmas—charity, good will, faith, love—are in fact eternal truths, necessary for a fulfilling life.

Despite its title and despite the very affecting moments of magic and happiness in the film, *One Magic Christmas* is realistic in a way that few Christmas movies are; it's about real people with very real problems. As critic David Edelstein wrote in *The Village Voice* (December 3, 1985), "It takes a lot of courage in the current market to make a Christmas film about real economic hardship and the effect of those woes on family life." It is, of course, that very realism that makes the film so effective: We sense that if a little Christmas magic can come into the lives of these plain, unpretentious, troubled people, it can come into ours as well. The best Christmas movies offer messages of hope; seldom has that message been more convincing than in this rewarding, tough-minded, sentimental—in the very best meaning of that word—movie.

One Magic Christmas was cofinanced by Disney and Telefilm Canada. The project was enthusiastically supported by Mary Steenbergen, the only "name" in the cast, and was probably produced only because she stuck with it. "I love the whole feeling of the script," she said at the time. "It's evocative of what Capra used to do, taking the reality of lower middle-class life in America and then putting a brush of magic across it."

Director Phillip Borsos said that he worked for nearly a decade to bring the film to the screen. "I wanted to do a Christmas story," he said, "because I basically believe the world is full of good people."

As *One Magic Christmas* ends, things are not substantially brighter for the Grainger family—they don't suddenly inherit a fortune or land great jobs. Their Christmas is just about what it would have been. The only thing that has changed is their spirit, particularly Ginnie's. Screenwriter Thomas Meehan said this was precisely the point. "I believe," he said, "in Santa Claus, or at least in the nice spirit that gets into the air around Christmas time. This film is trying to distill the spirit of Christmas while attacking commercialism."

The production, filmed on location in Toronto, Scarborough, Owen Sound, and Meaford in Canada, was plagued by unpredictable weather. There was no snow where they needed it, in the "snow belt" towns of Owen Sound and Meaford. Crews had to find snow elsewhere and haul it in—100 truckloads' worth. No sooner had this been done than a blizzard hit, forcing the crew to try to get rid of much of the snow they had gathered. After that, over the course of two weeks, came rain, fog, sleet, the year's worst blizzard, and high winds. Vehicles got mired in mud, snow drifts piled up to fifteen feet, and the visibility was sometimes zero.

Most of the interiors in the film were shot on real locations, but production designer Bill Brodie also built three major sets for *One Magic Christmas*: the Grainger house, the home of Jack's grandfather (Arthur Hill), and Santa's North Pole headquarters. The workshop was decorated with a collection of dolls, trains, and toys valued at $1 million. Santa's workers were costumed by Olga Dimitrov in a variety of clothing styles from the 1750s through the 1980s, supporting the pleasing idea that good people are rewarded with an afterlife in Santa's workshop.

In Santa's mail room, an unending stream of letters to Santa pours from a chute thirty feet above the floor. The Toronto Post Office helped with this particular illusion by contributing 20,000 real letters to Santa.

Production completed on April 10, 1985, and the film was released the following November, just in time for Christmas. *One Magic Christmas* did only marginally well at the box office—perhaps because word of mouth was that it was a serious and depressing film, not simple and colorful holiday fun. It got generally respectable reviews, though. Janet Maslin, of *The New York Times* (November 22, 1985) wrote that it was an "affecting, well-played film" and that Phillip Borsos "has a gravity here that at first seems decidedly un-Christmasy. But his solemnity is credible and appealing, and it ripens, slowly but surely, into a charmingly seasonal brand of childlike wonder."

One Magic Christmas has somehow never become the Christmas classic that it deserves to be; perhaps the first three-quarters of the film are simply too convincingly authentic in its portrayal of Christmas trauma. But for those who stay with it, *One Magic Christmas* becomes as moving as any other film of the season, and far more rewarding and memorable than most.

Santa Claus (Jan Rubes) presents Abbie with a special Christmas letter.

The Grainger children and their father journey home.

Abbie and her brother help decorate the tree.

Ernest Saves Christmas (1988)

CRITICS AND AUDIENCES don't always see eye to eye.

When actor Jim Varney brought his character, Ernest P. Worrell, to the big screen in *Ernest Goes to Camp* (1987), the reviews were, to put it mildly, savage. *Box Office* magazine called it "appalling," and a movie guide said that the film was "aimed at children who aren't very bright."

Ernest P. Worrel (Jim Varney) in *Ernest Saves Christmas*.

But moviegoers responded to its broad, slapstick-soaked humor, and *Ernest Goes to Camp* earned a respectable $20 million at the box office. In Hollywood, success breeds imitation, so Touchstone Pictures immediately began casting about for another Ernest movie. They found it in a script that had not been intended as anything of the sort.

Screenwriter-director Thom Eberhart (*Night of the Comet*, *Without a Clue*, *Captain Ron*) had earlier been asked by Disney (which owns Touchstone) to do a script rewrite. Eberhardt later told a reporter, "They had an original script with the concept of Santa Claus retiring. They wanted to do a Christmas story with Santa and adults." When Eberhardt turned in his rewrite, he said, "Disney flipped over it. They said, 'We're going to make the movie right now. We like everything about this, but we're going to set it in Orlando and turn it into an Ernest movie.'" *Ernest Saves Christmas* was born.

Ernest P. Worrell first saw the light of day in a long and profitable series of television commercials. A dim-bulb hick with a highly inflated opinion of his own intellect and a penchant for long and rambling flights of fancy that make sense only to himself, Ernest was best known for talking directly into the camera to his always unseen friend Vern. As played by the rubber-faced Varney, Ernest was funny in a way that completely avoided subtlety. His takes were always as big as possible, and the situations he found himself in were designed for maximum mayhem.

As *Ernest Saves Christmas* begins, Ernest is a cab driver whose driving skills are roughly on a par with his intellect. Taking a passenger to the airport, Ernest manages to lose him once, then deliver him in a catatonic state to the passenger zone, where the unlucky man falls onto the luggage conveyor belt and disappears into the system.

Also arriving at the Orlando Airport at about the same time is none other than Santa Claus (Douglas Seale)—or, as Ernest will call him, "His Big Red One-ness—the

Claus!" After over 100 years at the job, he's ready to pass the torch to another Santa, and he has picked a poor children's show host, Joe Carruthers (Oliver Clark), as his successor. Of course, once Santa becomes mixed up with Ernest, complications arise.

Although it's clear from the start that *Ernest Saves Christmas* wasn't written by Oscar Wilde (it's actually credited to Bonnie and Terry Turner, and Eberhardt's name is nowhere to be found), it is also not the abomination that many of its harshest critics claimed. Not only is

While Santa (Douglas Steele) and his successor (Oliver Clark) look on, Ernest demonstrates his reindeer skills in *Ernest Saves Christmas*.

Ernest P. Worrel (Jim Varney) helps out Santa's elves (Buddy Douglas and Patty Maloney) in *Ernest Saves Christmas*.

there something endearing about its relentless, low-budget stupidity, but it also comes up with a few neat variations on Christmas themes.

For example, in most Santa films, Saint Nick carries a large sack bulging with toys. In *Ernest Saves Christmas*, the bag is filled with magical light, which only becomes a toy when it's pulled out. Since Santa knows what every boy and girl wants, the magic light "becomes" that toy on Christmas morning. But it doesn't work for anybody else: When Ernest tries it, the light simply becomes a pink flamingo or some other tasteless and tacky, Ernest-appropriate gift.

So that everything will be ready for the new Santa to take over his duties on Christmas Eve, Santa has had the sleigh and reindeer shipped to the airport depot to await pickup by two elves. The reindeer don't like being confined to their crates, however, and kick their way out, then fly up to the ceiling and mill around up there.

Ernest Saves Christmas also has a little fun with the *Silent Night, Deadly Night* type of Christmas horror film. Joe Carruthers is auditioning for a movie to be called *Christmas Slay*, in which an alien comes to earth on Christmas Eve to start killing and maiming. When Joe objects to the bad language and violence in the film, the moviemakers think he's crazy, but that just confirms to Santa that Joe is the right fellow to take on the job of Father Christmas.

The last act of the film is taken up with a frantic sleigh flight—steered by Ernest with much the same skill as when he drives a cab—and the clearing up of several dangling plot points. Although the final scenes never become genuinely moving in ways that the filmmakers clearly intended, there is a kind of sweet, touching quality to the moments when Joe becomes transformed into Santa Claus and heads off into the night, Ernest by his side.

Ernest Saves Christmas met with about the same kind of critical response as *Ernest Goes to Camp*. And it also performed very well at the box office. One clue to its success is that there have been no fewer than seven more sequels: *Ernest Goes to Jail* (1990), *Ernest Scared Stupid* (1991), *Ernest Rides Again* (1993), *Ernest Goes to School* (1994), *Slam Dunk Ernest* (1995), *Ernest in the Army* (1997), and *Ernest Goes to Africa* (1997). It's safe to say that all nine of the films put together have never generated a single positive review. But for someone seeking an uncomplicated good time, obvious gags, and no pretensions, Ernest P. Worrell is always there to oblige.

Is *Ernest Saves Christmas* a great Christmas movie? No, but it's a *genuine* Christmas movie, with plenty of heart, if not much brains.

National Lampoon's Christmas Vacation (1989)

National Lampoon's Christmas Vacation is the third of four (so far) cinematic holidays with the disaster-prone Griswold family, a series that also includes *National Lampoon's Vacation* (1983), *National Lampoon's European Vacation* (1985), and *National Lampoon's Vegas Vacation* (1997).

Clark (Chevy Chase), the head of the clan, is an earnest dimwit; his wife, Ellen (Beverly D'Angelo), is sweet and

Beaming with the Christmas spirit, Clark Griswold (Chevy Chase) carves the turkey for his family—*clockwise from bottom:* Aunt Bethany (Mae Questel); Clark Sr. (John Randolph); Clark's mother, Nora (Diane Ladd); his wife, Ellen (Beverly D'Angelo); Ellen's father, Art (E.G. Marshall); Ellen's mother, Francis (Doris Roberts); and Clark's cousin, Eddie (Randy Quaid)—in *National Lampoon's Christmas Vacation*.

forgiving; and the kids–Juliette Lewis and Johnny Galecki in this version–are typical teenagers, fairly contemptuous of their parents but fond of them nonetheless.

The humor in the *Vacation* films runs the gamut from obvious and juvenile to genuinely clever. There is rarely anything subtle about the antics of the Griswolds–Clark exists within a perpetual pratfall–but when the films work, they can be sidesplitting.

Christmas Vacation is among the funniest entries in the series. And it has another element, too–sentiment. Clark Griswold genuinely longs to give his family a warm, happy, old-fashioned Christmas. In some ways, he does, despite a crashing series of misadventures that include an exploding Christmas tree, an electrocuted cat, and more fallings off roofs, crashing through windows, and getting conked on the heads than any five Three Stooges shorts could boast. Ladders collapse under Clark, he drives his station wagon under a huge logging truck, and he becomes the unwilling passenger on a sled that zooms down the steepest hill on the map. But he is also a man who, trapped and freezing in the attic, threads up his old home movies and weeps with nostalgia at what he believes to have been a happy childhood—with loving holidays of the sort that he now wants *his* family to share.

Despite all the breakage and bone-crunching stunts, Clark's biggest pain comes from the avalanche of family members that crashes down upon him—his parents (John Randolph and Diane Ladd), Ellen's parents (E. G. Marshall and Doris Roberts), weird Uncle Lewis (William Hickey) and Aunt Bethany (Mae Questel, beloved by cartoon fans as the original voice of both Betty Boop and Olive Oyl). Neither Aunt Bethany nor Uncle Lewis are playing with a full deck. When asked to say grace, the only thing Aunt Bethany can come up with is the Pledge of Allegiance, which everyone dutifully recites with her. Uncle Lewis steps away from the holiday table for a quick smoke in the living room and sets fire to the Christmas tree, which explodes so quickly in a fireball that no one but Clark even notices.

Chevy Chase and Randy Quaid in *National Lampoon's Christmas Vacation*.

But most horrifying of all is the arrival of Clark's lout of a cousin, Eddie (Randy Quaid), his wife (Miriam Flynn), and their two kids. Eddie is a slob, a freeloader, a hick—and somehow, one of the film's most endearing characters.

Christmas Vacation was directed by Jeremiah Chechik, a former commercial director making his feature debut. He took cast and crew to Breckenridge, Colorado, filling three hotels with his army of filmmakers. As always seems to happen on movies set in the wintertime, the weather turned unseasonably warm as soon as they arrived, necessitating the hauling of huge truckloads of snow from one side of town to the other. And as soon as this was accomplished, it started snowing again, giving Chechik and crew seventy-seven inches in less than a week.

The scene in which Clark rode down the hill on a sled was shot—at night—at an altitude of 11,000 feet, with the wind chill dipping the temperature below zero. Some crew members were hospitalized with hypothermia and altitude sickness.

Other scenes filmed in Breckenridge include one in which Clark drives his station wagon off the road and flies

The Griswold family—*from left to right:* Rusty (Johnny Galecki), Audrey (Juliette Lewis), Clark (Chevy Chase), and Ellen (Beverly D'Angelo)—in *National Lampoon's Christmas Vacation.*

through the air before setting down near a Christmas Tree Ranch. This "flying" stunt was shot with three cameras, and one take, at the Breckenridge Golf Course, designed–probably for other purposes–by legendary golf pro Jack Nicklaus. And when Chechik needed to film a scene of Clark and Eddie out shopping, he simply took Chase and Quaid to a local Wal-Mart and filmed among the ordinary shoppers.

The Griswold house and neighborhood stood on Burbank's Warner Ranch. The residential street, used in the thirties and forties for the popular *Blondie* series starring Arthur Lake and Penny Singleton, is still known as the "Blondie Street." Although it was springtime in California, the Blondie Street was transformed—via cotton batting, bleached sawdust, and sparkles—into a Winter Wonderland.

Finally, the company moved over to the Warner Bros. Studio in Burbank to film the interiors of the Griswold house on two large soundstages. Chevy Chase recalls shooting the scenes in the attic as being the most unpleasant moments of the film—the tiny set was hot, claustrophobic, and filled with atmosphere smoke.

National Lampoon's Christmas Vacation was released in late November 1989, just in time for the Christmas season. The critics were not quite overwhelmed. Janet Maslin wrote in *The New York Times* (December 1, 1989), "The film looks tacky, what with flimsy props and occasionally blurry cinematography, and the direction of Jeremiah S. Chechik displays comic timing that is uncertain at best. In spite of all this, however, the Griswolds do occasionally have their moments."

Michael Wilmington, in the *Los Angeles Times* (December 1, 1989), called the film "sometimes funny, sometimes tasteless." He adds, "This hideous vision of a suburban Christmas gone totally amok is typical of [writer-producer John] Hughes, encased in a sentimental overview—like a Norman Rockwell portrait with a punk rock backbeat, and spiders nibbling through the frame." *

But despite the critics, audiences responded enthusiastically, turning *Christmas Vacation* into a real hit at the box office. The film has only gained in stature over the years, taking on the sheen of something close to a genuine Christmas classic. Video stores report that it is consistently among the most popular rentals during the Christmas season, and it has inspired rabid fans of the sort who memorize every line, pratfall, and sound effect.

---

* John Hughes is a writer, producer, and director with, it seems, a particular fondness for the holidays. In addition to *Christmas Vacation*, Hughes wrote and produced the Christmas-themed *Home Alone* (1990), *Home Alone 2: Lost in New York* (1992), and a remake of *Miracle on 34th Street*. Hughes also wrote, produced, and directed *Planes, Trains and Automobiles* (1987) and wrote and produced *Dutch* (1991), both of which are about people trying to get home for Thanksgiving. There are, in addition, numerous holiday references in many other Hughes films.

Chevy Chase Remembers
National Lampoon's Christmas Vacation

✦ ✦ ✦

The movie is about all of the Christmas vacations that we all have when our parents and family members come and visit us, where you don't go away. You don't go to Florida. You don't go to Disneyland. You don't go to ski. You stay home and everybody comes and visits. And the idea came about partially through a concept that I had—because this is the way we have our Christmases at our house. My wife's parents come and

Chevy Chase in *National Lampoon's Christmas Vacation*.

there's twenty people, family. And her father smokes, and I just had this vision of him leaving the table in the middle of Christmas dinner and hearing a kind of a WHOOSH [as the Christmas tree goes up in smoke, as it does in the film]. I'm giggling to myself talking to [producers] John Hughes and Mark Canton over at Warner's about this concept, this physical gag of my getting up from the table to just check it out and seeing that the tree now is just nothing, just black. And [the father] is black [with soot]–you know how if you don't water a tree on Christmas and there's fire anywhere near it, the whole house goes up.

So that joke was sort of the beginning of a series of concepts that came about, all related to the earlier National Lampoon *Vacation* movies. You know, can we bring Cousin Eddie in? Can we bring the various characters that we used in other *Vacation* movies? And we can bring in Ellen's parents and bring Clark's parents and see how it goes and how many other jokes we can get? And we began to talk more and more about other ideas, like where do you get your tree from? Well, everybody usually goes to a tree lot, a place down on the corner. But we're going to really do it Griswold style and go out to the woods and cut our own, and joke after joke happens.

Then the idea was to bring to mind a normal American family Christmas but with all of the possible things that can go wrong. Too much food. Too much of the same food. Too many people. Arguments. All the crap that gets in the way of the religious experience, the sacred experience of the family being together. And so *Christmas Vacation* is about those three or four days of Christmas.

Clark Griswold is a character I portrayed in a couple other pictures before that, in other *Vacation* projects. He's a family man who is bent on making his children's childhoods better than his own–and also bringing back good memories of his own childhood, of staying a child, but providing them with great experiences of the past and those that he missed, that didn't happen for him. And he's an optimist and yet things continue to go wrong. But he's the kind of guy that stays on top of it, trying to stay close to the family. He screws up a lot.

Clark's family views him, I think, as an idiot, but I think they love him. You know, there's always Russ and Audrey [Clark's son and daughter]. Those characters have changed in every movie. Their ages change: They get younger, they get older, they get younger again. Clark is always turning around and saying, "Russ, oh there you are." And he's always there. I think they view Clark as a bit of a doofus. And I think that Ellen [Clark's wife], the character that Beverly D'Angelo plays, views him as kindhearted, good-hearted, well-meaning—but a catastrophe.

I think one of my favorite scenes was just the eating sequence, because you know how you wait all day. You can't wait for that turkey, even though you've had Thanksgiving, and it's that season of putting on ten pounds. But you wait all day for that wonderful turkey and gravy, potatoes, and cranberry sauce, and somebody's always brought something to the table. There's always an extra kind of potato. You have sweet potatoes, and you have mashed potatoes and baked, a hundred different kinds of potatoes. Potato salad. The carving of the turkey is a big deal. Well, what I wanted to do was at one point cover just the eating sequence. You know, we say grace and then we eat. And I suggested to the director [Jeremiah Chechik] that we try this steadicam, hand-held shot going just around the table watching this family of, I guess, fifteen, or whatever it turned into by then, eat. And to me that's one of my favorite scenes, and it culminates, of course, in the tree exploding. There's also the cat, which is one of my favorites, too. The cat gnaws at the Christmas tree lights and gets electrocuted.

The effort to light houses, I've seen this go on in Middle America all my life, but I've seen it go on much more since we made the movie, even. People really make an effort, particularly out here in California where you don't have snow. Lighting the house in a merry fashion and one that celebrates both Christmas and the birth of Christ. As many lights as you can get on—that scene to me is one of my favorites. I mean, there are many scenes in that movie that make me laugh. And you know I could go on and on because every year it's on television and every time I get a chance to peek at it here and there, I see a scene that I remember shooting. I think they're all so reminiscent of Christmases we've all had. Hiding presents, buying the wrong thing, waiting for your Christmas bonus, all of those issues that are on the minds of most Americans.

We began shooting in Breckenridge, Colorado, just to get snow for the finding of the Christmas tree, the Griswold family Christmas tree. And it was already mid- to late March. They were a little bit afraid we might not get any snow, but at the ski resort, we figured, well, we're high enough. We were at 12,000, 13,000 feet. And suddenly we ended up with eight feet of snow—a blizzard. So that made it very difficult, and we had to go inside to shoot some scenes—a rain set, whatever you want to call it. It's a covered set, basically, in a gym where we built the attic to the house, in which Clark Griswold gets stuck and watches old movies of himself and ultimately falls through the floor. That was very difficult. It was dusty. We needed a lot of smoke for the smoke effect of a dusty attic. People were coughing and vomiting and—I don't know if they were vomiting but they were pretty ill. And their eyes were red and that was typical.

We had some trouble with some of the gags that required fire, explosions, and things of that nature. I think the most difficult parts of the movie were for the director who had never really directed a picture. And he was a commercial director named Jeremiah Chechik, and he was wonderful. He had exactly the right spirit and a great musical sense of what kind of songs to use. But he also had in a small set and one living room, basically, some of the great actors of our time—E. G. Marshall, John Randolph, Diane Ladd, Doris Roberts, and a number of people whom he had expected would simply step on their marks and do the lines. And that was a little bit difficult because I had to explain to him one evening that really you want an actor to be able to run through the scene a few times with other actors. And then after they've rehearsed it a few times, you can determine what there is you can use of their ideas, where they're moving, and where they aren't. How many setups that takes, all those issues. So that was difficult. And I think it was a little tough on Jeremiah. But by and large, it went quite smoothly.

Oh, I know what was tough—the sledding scene. I had to go through the woods in Breckenridge at about four in the morning for about a week on a sled that had been put on a track, but there was no slowing that thing up. And that was frightening and that was a tough one. And people were getting altitude sickness, crew members. There were two or three production assistants who would get altitude sickness. This is about twenty or thirty below zero. It's two or three in the morning and suddenly we'd be missing a production assistant, they had simply wandered off in a T-shirt into the woods in some sort of narcosis or whatever they call it–nitrogen narcosis, like you get underwater. That was something. And I remember a few of them had to be helicoptered out.

I think the difference between *Christmas Vacation* and great movies like *It's a Wonderful Life*–although I don't mean to label *It's a Wonderful Life* and others as being "sentimental"–is that we never looked for sentimentality. Sentiment's fine. It's sentimentality that goes against my nature in doing satire. I think it depends on what you're trying to do. If you're pandering and if you're really trying to cull a tear, the audience can see through that. I don't think sentiment is essential, although I must admit in the end, the idea is getting your wish. The idea is that the children are happy and that everybody gets what they want. But there are degrees of sentiment and there are degrees of pathos, you know, and it depends on what you're looking for, what the story is about. Most Christmas movies are not "about Christmas," but the classic *Christmas Carol* is about honor, is about forgiveness, is about caring about others, and it's about giving. Those elements I think are important in a picture that's about Christmas.

And certainly those elements are there in *Christmas Vacation*. I think so, yeah. There's no question that Clark Griswold cares a great deal about making it a great Christmas. The question is, how shallow is he? And does he really know what that is? But in the end, you know, it's not just about [how] his paycheck isn't enough; it's did he give his family a good Christmas? They were all together in the house–that's an important thing. Things that we overlook. We generally leave mom's house, or whoever you're visiting over Christmas, and there were so many things that were a pain in the ass, but the things that stay with you are almost subconscious and subliminal, and they have to do with that rebirth and that sense of the family being together again.

In fact, watching movies is not part of our tradition any more than reading *The Night Before Christmas* is. I've got three children, and the tradition is really to try to get them to bed and do the Santa thing. And I don't know who's reading this. I don't want to give any secrets away to children, but you know it's a very busy, busy evening. And in the morning, the kids are up real early, three, four, five–whenever that sun's up or whenever they wake up and they want to see if Santa came–and I make a major effort to make it look good. Lots of fingerprints, cookies eaten, milk drunk, things spilled, all of that stuff that makes it magic for children.

Why is the movie still so popular? *National Lampoon's Christmas Vacation* is funny, and it's classic as a comedy of errors. And it's just got wonderful moments that people don't forget. And you're asking the guy who sort of half wrote it and starred in it and had a big part in directing it, and it's hard for me to answer that. It is clearly popular and people like it. And I don't know what it is. I'd have to give a lot of credit to the way it looks and the way the music seems to match our nostalgia from generations ago. I mean, you hear Gene Autry singing "Here Comes Santa Claus" juxtaposed against the police showing up.

But it still brings together many generations. It has a lot of nostalgic properties. And a lot of it's exterior at night, and it has a wonderful bluish sort of tint to it that's warm and hospitable and makes you want to watch more. You never quite know what else is going to happen, what else is going to go wrong.

Indeed, it's easy to see how *National Lampoon's Christmas Vacation* has inspired such loyalty. It is truly funny—one of those films that seems to get funnier on repeat viewings—but it is also quite touching. It is significant that the film doesn't end on a big laugh line or some other kind of topper, but on the beatific face of Clark Griswold gazing heavenward, smiling with slightly dazed delight that his Christmas holiday—as fraught with disaster as it was—actually turned out all right.

Daniel Stern (*left*) and Joe Pesci in *Home Alone*.

Home Alone (1990) and *Home Alone 2: Lost in New York* (1992)

Home Alone is one of the most wildly successful comedies of the nineties, a frantic cartoon filled with pratfalls, sight gags, and all the color and tinsel of a beautiful, though slightly explosive, Christmas present. Director Chris Columbus (who also wrote the Christmas-themed *Gremlins*) said that he set the film during the holiday season for a reason. "I wanted to do a Christmas film," he said. "I like to set films at Christmas because, visually, they look terrific. In a Christmas picture, there's something warm about seeing snow."

Columbus and screenwriter-producer John Hughes found that snow—and plenty of it—in the Chicago area beginning in February 1990. The company filmed in Kenilworth, Winnetka, Wilmette, and Evanston. Special effects supervisor Bill Purcell, however, said that Mother Nature wasn't always cooperative. "There was no end to what would happen," he said. "The winter would come, then we would have a heat wave, so we kept having to put the snow in or take it out." He and his crew used 360 tons of shaved ice, 6,250 yards of snow blanket, 11,000 gallons of airport runway foam, 6,000 pounds of potato flakes, 1,000 pounds of minifibers, and 900 pounds of polyurethane snow.

Macaulay Culkin (*left*) in *Home Alone* with Joe Pesci.

Over the course of production, Columbus and his cast and crew filmed at Chicago's O'Hare Airport (which also stood in for Paris's Orly Airport), Winnetka's City Hall,

Grace Episcopal Church in Oak Park, and New Trier West High School in Northfield, where temporary soundstages were created in vacant gymnasiums.

Home Alone is essentially two Christmas movies in one. The most immediate of those movies is the one about eight-year-old Kevin (Macaulay Culkin) who is accidentally left behind when his large extended family leaves for a trip to Paris. Two dim-bulb burglars (Joe Pesci and Daniel Stern) target houses that they know to be empty for the Christmas holidays, but they don't count on the tenacious Kevin, who sets a series of boobie traps for them—traps of a variety and complexity that would bewilder a Green Beret. The burglars' assault on the house brings *Home Alone* to a fever pitch of Road Runner-style violence in which Kevin shoots, burns, and bonks the empty-headed crooks—and they just keep coming back for more mayhem.

Macaulay Culkin stars in *Home Alone*.

The other Christmas movie in *Home Alone* is a tender, surprisingly touching meditation on loneliness and the loss of family. Kevin is at first euphoric at his freedom, believing that he actually wished his sometimes annoying family to disappear. Soon enough, he starts to bait them, eating enormous sundaes and watching bad crime movies, hoping to do something bad enough to make his parents show up again.

Living next door to Kevin is his counterpart in old age, the mysterious man with a very Christmasy name, Mr. Marley (Roberts Blossom). The neighborhood kids have concocted a gruesome past for the old man, and Kevin screams in fear every time Marley looks at him. But when they meet in church on Christmas Eve and begin to talk, Kevin learns that Marley is estranged from his own family after a major argument; both Kevin and Marley are "home alone."

Home Alone became a true phenomenon upon its original release, selling $68.9 million worth of tickets in its first nineteen days of release. The success was mostly due to the uproarious slapstick that dominates the final third of the film. But those quiet moments with Mr. Marley give *Home Alone* its heart. At the end, Kevin is reunited with his own family, but there isn't a fraction of the emotion in that reunion as in the one Kevin sees from his window, when Mr. Marley happily embraces his granddaughter, as his son and daughter-in-law look on. It is this moment that makes *Home Alone* a true Christmas movie, instead of simply a movie set at Christmas. The violent moments and wild comedy could have taken place at any time, but the scenes with Marley are *about* Christmas and the season's inspiration of forgiveness and rebirth.

The incredible success of *Home Alone* made talk of a sequel inevitable. "I have more things I could do with Kevin's character," John Hughes said at the time. "There's

"The Wet Bandits," Harry (Joe Pesci, *left*) and Marv (Daniel Stern, *right*) battle with Kevin McCallister in *Home Alone 2: Lost in New York*.

Marv (Daniel Stern, *left*) and Harry (Joe Pesci, *right*) are up to no good in *Home Alone 2: Lost in New York*.

room for another chapter. I think everyone wants to make it." Oddly, in light of the plentiful—if comic—chaos and pain that permeate the film, Hughes said that he believed the popularity of the movie stemmed from the fact that "it's warm and funny. Warm and funny is sort of becoming scarce in the real world. Violence is taking over."

As Hughes promised, the sequel to *Home Alone* was in the works in no time. This time, the family is heading off to Florida for Christmas. Kevin somehow manages to get on the wrong plane and ends up—alone, but not at home—in New York City. Hence the title, *Home Alone 2: Lost in New York*.

Home Alone 2 brought back virtually the entire cast of the first film, including John Heard and Catherine O'Hara as Kevin's parents, and Pesci and Stern as the two crooks. By a strange coincidence, they are in New York with plans to rob the city's largest toy store on Christmas Eve. And who should they run into on the streets of that huge, crowded metropolis? One guess.

The violence in *Home Alone 2* is, if anything, even more extreme than in the first film. Critic Nancy Blaine, writing in the *Village View* (November 20-26, 1992), said that this time, "Kevin succeeds less as a Shirley Temple-cute Roadrunner substitute than as a borderline psychopath. The fault lies with director Chris Columbus and screenwriter John Hughes, who have transferred animated sadism into a family-oriented feature without taking the live-action law of gravity into effect: physical comedy stops being funny when it looks like it could kill, or means to."

Kate (Catherine O'Hara) in *Home Alone 2: Lost in New York*. Also starring John Heard as Peter and Macaulay Culkin as Kevin.

The main problem with *Home Alone 2* is that it feels less like a sequel than a remake. Kevin befriended poor Mr. Marley next-door in the first film, and Mr. Marley stepped in at the climax to save Kevin from the thugs. In the sequel, he befriends a poor homeless woman (Brenda Fricker), who steps in at the climax to...well, you know.

Unfortunately, what worked as genuine, tender sentiment in *Home Alone*, seems like calculated tear-jerking smarminess in the sequel. The second go-around was indeed successful (*Home Alone 3* came along in 1997), but it wasn't a phenomenon. Perhaps this is because even those who enjoyed it most felt as though they had seen it all before.

A Midnight Clear (1991)

A Midnight Clear is one of the most powerful antiwar movies ever made, a minor classic that was barely noticed upon its release in 1991. William Wharton, the author best known for *Birdy*, wrote the novel on which the film was based, and his vision was admirably served by Keith Gordon's adaptation. Gordon, an actor-turned filmmaker (who appeared in eighties horror movies *Dressed to Kill* and *Christine*), also directed *A Midnight Clear*, assembling a talented cast including Ethan Hawke, Gary Sinise, Peter Berg, Frank Whaley, Arye Gross, John McGinley, and Kevin Dillon (the latter two veterans of Oliver Stone's *Platoon*).

The setting is Christmas 1944 in the Ardennes Forest on the French-German border during the last days of

World War II. Baby-faced sergeant Will Knott (Ethan Hawke) narrates the story of an intelligence and reconnaissance squad composed of high IQ "whiz kids." The squad has been decimated by a bloody "map inspired" military maneuver orchestrated by regimental commander Griffin (McGinley), who is, ironically, a mortician in civilian life. Griffin sends the I-and-R squad to occupy an abandoned chateau near the front in an intelligence-gathering mission.

Hawke's evocative narration introduces us to the platoon—Avakian (Dillon); Shutzer (Gross); Miller (Berg); "Father," the chaplain (Whaley); and "Mother" Wilkins (Sinise), an emotionally scarred neurotic. Through flashbacks, we see various scenes: the squad's training days as fresh-faced recruits; a poignant episode when Will, Avakian, Shutzer, and Berg attempt to lose their virginity; and the horrible death of a comrade in a field hospital.

Left to right: Kevin Dillion, Peter Berg, Arye Gross, Ethan Hawke, Frank Whaley, and Gary Sinise in *A Midnight Clear.*

Hawke and his men discover a group of German soldiers near the chateau and prepare for a fight. Over the course of several nights, they realize that these "enemies" are as war weary as they are. Only a few yards apart one night, the Germans start hurling snowballs instead of ordnance at the GIs. On another bitterly cold evening, the Germans erect a crude Christmas tree in a cemetery, and the Americans join them to celebrate with Christmas carols. The Germans wish to surrender but insist on staging a fake skirmish so that their families won't be punished for their cowardice. The GIs agree to the plan, which goes terribly wrong.

Director Gordon peppers the film with memorable moments—the squad encountering two soldiers frozen to death; a beautiful winterscape, with a frozen hand sticking out of the snow; two GIs dancing to "The Jersey Bounce." One scene in particular—a deer coming out of the chateau when the men first approach the house, rifles at the ready—brings poetry (and Christmas symbols) to an otherwise familiar war scene. Throughout the film, the director masterfully captures life in the field, the

Ethan Hawke in *A Midnight Clear.*

Left to right: Peter Berg, Arye Gross, Kevin Dillon, Frank Whaley, and Ethan Hawke in *A Midnight Clear*.

Gary Sinise plays "Mother" Wilkins in *A Midnight Clear*.

privation and the profanity, the soldiers' fear and their will to survive.

Filmed near Park City, Utah, the production also benefits from Mark Isham's haunting score and Tom Richmond's cinematography, which creates a black-and-white-in-color effect with its stark images of snowy landscape. Emotionally and visually, *A Midnight Clear* lives up to the power and the passion of the best World War II films, such as Ford's *They Were Expendable*, Milestone's *A Walk in the Sun*, Wellman's *The Story of G. I. Joe* and *Battleground*, and Fuller's *The Big Red One*. Well-received by the critics, *A Midnight Clear* was poorly released but has a growing reputation thanks to video and cable television. As the nineties come to a close, the picture will undoubtedly prove to be one of the decade's finest films—and a very different kind of Christmas movie.

J.A.G.

The Santa Clause (1994)

THE MORAL of this movie is if Santa Claus ever falls off your roof and you find his calling card, read the fine print.

Near the beginning of *The Santa Clause*, Scott Calvin (Tim Allen), and his son, Charlie (Eric Lloyd), hear a clatter on the roof on Christmas Eve. Scott rushes out to find Santa standing at the chimney, and when Scott yells at him, Santa loses his balance and comes crashing to the ground. Looking for identification, Scott finds a card that reads: "Santa Claus, North Pole." On the other side is written, "If you put on the suit, the reindeer will know what to do." To their amazement, Scott and Charlie see that there are indeed reindeer, and a sled, on the roof. Being a pragmatist, Scott just wants to assume that the whole thing is a hallucination, but Charlie urges him to put on the suit and see what happens.

What happens, of course, is that Scott Calvin literally starts to become Santa Claus, a turn of events that sends shock waves through his office and his relationships with his ex-wife, Laura (Wendy Crewson); her new husband, Neal (Judge Reinhold); and particularly, his son, Charlie.

Scott turns into Santa because he didn't read the fine print on the card–the "Santa clause"–which stipulates that whoever dons the suit and delivers the toys becomes the next Santa. In no time, Scott finds himself at the North Pole surrounded by elves.

Tim Allen stars as Santa Claus in *The Santa Clause.*

The Santa Clause shares a conceit with the earlier Disney film *Ernest Saves Christmas*–namely, that there is no one Santa Claus but an ongoing series of them. In *Ernest Saves Christmas*, Santa realizes that he has gotten too old for the job and has chosen his successor. In *The Santa Clause*, the old Santa has to retire due to illness–or maybe death. After he falls to the ground from Scott's roof, he simply disappears, leaving an empty suit for Scott to put on.

In fact, in the early drafts of the script, Santa's fall results in a broken neck, leaving him a crumpled, distorted heap on the ground. Tim Allen recalled, "John Pasquin, the director, said, 'It's a little grim, isn't it? To start a movie out with Santa breaking his neck?' And I went, 'I like it!' So it grabbed me right away."

Tim Allen speaks to an elf in *The Santa Clause.*

There were other dark elements in the earlier script as well. "It was going to be a black comedy," Allen said, "but as John [Pasquin] so brilliantly pointed out, 'It's got to go one way or the other. If it's a black comedy, then we should take the references to kids out of it and make the elves much more sinister than they are.' Because as we found out about elves in mythology, they're not very pleasant beings. The way they get more elves is kidnap children at night. And we both went, 'Well, we've got to skate over that little thing, don't we? Let's not bring that into it.'"

Pasquin agreed. "The first script was pretty dark—the delusionary quality of the character was explored a lot

Tim Allen takes over as Santa Claus with his son Charlie (Eric Lloyd) by his side in *The Santa Clause*.

An impromtu line of kids who want to talk to Santa in *The Santa Clause*.

more. In that version, they actually committed the character of Scott Calvin to an asylum, and eventually he escaped and became Santa Claus."

Pasquin continued, "When I first read it I found that there wasn't enough heart in the movie. Christmas movies to me have to have heart at the center. They have to be about something. I always felt that this was a story about a father and a child, and then, in the process, the father becomes Santa Claus. Also, I wanted to play up the fact that Scott wasn't chosen for this by accident. He was chosen to be Santa Claus because he needed to be Santa Claus... because he wasn't relating to his son, because he didn't listen to his son."

Scott Calvin, like Howard Langston (Arnold Schwarzenegger) in *Jingle All the Way* (1996), is a businessman whose success has distanced him from his family. In Scott's case, his type-A personality led to a divorce and to a strained relationship with his son, whom he doesn't quite understand. When Charlie is dropped off at Scott's on Christmas Eve, he urges his mother to pick him up as early as possible the next morning, as if dreading every minute he is forced to spend with his father.

That night, Scott—like all movie dads—burns the dinner,

and they have to go out to a fast food restaurant. Once there, they find that every other table is occupied by glum fathers and depressed kids–all there for the same reason.

The Santa Clause offers one refreshing variation on a movie cliche. Whereas the kids in, for example, *All I Want for Christmas* hate their new stepfather-to-be–and with good reason–Charlie gets along fine with his stepdad, Neal. Neal's problem is that, as a psychiatrist, he has lost his sense of whimsy along the way. He finds Charlie's total belief that his father is turning into Santa Claus to be dangerously delusional. Because he is sincere and rather humorless, Neal is an easy butt for Scott's wisecracks, but he is not simply a straw man to be kicked around for comic purposes.

Santa Claus (Tim Allen) and Charlie (Eric Lloyd) are ready for take-off in *The Santa Clause*.

Scott's transformation is physical first, and mental and emotional later. To his dismay, he finds that he is gaining weight rapidly–possibly due to his new diet of milk and cookies. His hair has turned white, and no matter how often he shaves, he still ends each day with a luxurious beard. All the other adults in his life–Laura and Neal, his boss Mr. Whittle (Peter Boyle), his office coworkers–are also concerned about the changes going on in Scott's life. But children know, instinctively and immediately, that he really is Santa–they know it, in fact, before Scott believes it himself. In one priceless scene, Scott is at the park watching Charlie play ball. A little girl stares closely at him, then sits on his lap and says, "I want a pair of ballet slippers." Soon, there is a line around the park of kids waiting patiently to talk with Santa.

Although set somewhere in Illinois (if the car license plates are any indication), *The Santa Clause* was filmed primarily in Ontario. The film is, of course, crammed with special effects of the flying-reindeer variety. Tim Allen himself became the focus of some of the most notable visual tricks. Early on, Scott Calvin learns just how Santa can get down a chimney of any size–or down no chimney at all. He

Santa Claus (Tim Allen) has trouble with a chimney in *The Santa Clause*.

simply contorts his body ("like Jello," as the film's special effects crew put it) and pours it into whatever opening is available. In the room that holds the Christmas tree, a large fireplace magically appears, long enough for Santa to enter and leave.

Later, as Scott tries desperately to retain his original looks while being taken over by Santa, Allen's image morphs from one look to the next—hair turning white and a long, full beard growing in the space of about two seconds.

These are the flashier visual effects, but the more subtle one is a bit more impressive. Special makeup artists Alec Gillis and Tom Woodruff Jr. created prosthetics to support the illusion that Scott has gained a hundred pounds. Woodruff said, "You're dealing with a human being [Tim Allen] that's worldwide known. And you're dealing with skin tones that have to look natural. He has to look believable—he can't be distracting to the audience." In some scenes Allen was equipped with a "fat suit" that weighed over thirty-five pounds.

For Scott Calvin's ultimate transformation into Santa Claus, the makeup artists studied early images of Saint Nick from the twenties and thirties, including some Norman Rockwell paintings. "We picked out the aspects of the face that we liked," Gillis said, " the sort of cherub quality, the forehead that pooches forward in sort of a babylike quality—because the transformation was always intended to be a pleasant one."

One of the reasons that *The Santa Clause* works so well is that it accomplishes two things at once: It's a comedy-fantasy about a man who turns into Santa Claus, has adventures at the North Pole, and flies around in a sleigh; it's also a pretty perceptive statement about how a father can—must—literally and figuratively transform himself into the kind, gentle, loving—and attentive—dad that he needs to be. Laura and Neal, convinced that Scott has gone crazy, petition for sole custody of Charlie, but it is really Scott who has to learn how to share his son with them. Although all ends happily with a fully functioning family unit—Neal included—this ending doesn't spring from fantasy but from the mature realization of all those involved that each member of the family has something important to contribute.

There are big laughs in *The Santa Clause*, but there is a feeling of tenderness, too; the climax offers the kind of triumphant moment of joy that can move audiences to laughter and tears at the same moment. For this—and for its precise grasp on both the exhilaration of fantasy and the very real need for family and security—*The Santa Clause* is definitely a great Christmas movie.

Howard Langston (Arnold Schwarzenegger) promises his son, Jamie (Jake Lloyd), that he will buy him the most sought-after toy of the season in *Jingle All the Way*.

Jingle All the Way (1996)

THE CLASSIC Christmas movies of the thirties and forties concentrated on lessons of hope and the Christmas spirit; *It's a Wonderful Life*, *Miracle on 34th Street*, and *The Bishop's Wife* are stories of faith reclaimed and families reborn—warm, inspiring, and moving stories of the magic of Christmas.

Those themes are present in *Jingle All the Way*, too, but this film has less to do with Christmas sentiment than it does with the sometimes unbearable stresses and expectations of the season. In *Jingle All the Way*, two fathers, played by Arnold Schwarzenegger and Sinbad, find themselves in a situation that most parents will find all too plausible. It is Christmas Eve, and they are both desperately trying to buy the latest hot toy for their kids—a Turbo Man action figure. The only trouble is, all the Turbo Man dolls have been sold out since Thanksgiving.

This presents a double-pronged problem for Howard Langston (Schwarzenegger): He has been so consumed with business lately that he has ignored his wife, Liz (Rita Wilson), and son, Jamie (Jake Lloyd). Time and again he has made promises to them that he has failed to keep. As the film opens, he encounters a host of difficulties on his way to Jamie's karate class award ceremony—and misses it altogether. Apologizing later, he tells his son that he will make it up to him by getting him anything he wants for Christmas. What Jamie wants, of course, is a Turbo Man action figure, based on a wildly popular television superhero. No problem, Howard says. Even when Liz reminds him that he was supposed to have picked up the toy weeks earlier, Howard is unconcerned and heads out first thing on the morning of Christmas Eve to pick one up.

Howard Langston (Arnold Schwarzenegger) battles a pint-sized Santa (Vern Troyer).

The pesky postal worker Myron Larabee (Sinbad) in *Jingle All the Way*.

Of course, the first store he goes to has no Turbo Man figures—the employees break into hysterical laughter when they learn that Howard thinks he's going to find one—and Howard spends the rest of the day getting into violent and outrageous scrapes, without getting any closer to achieving his goal.

Schwarzenegger said, "It is every man's story. All fathers want to be heroes in the eyes of their kids. And we've taken that simple fact a step further, placing it into the context of two things all parents—including me—have gone through: finding the latest, hottest toy for their kids, and juggling a private and professional life."

There is a recurring image in Christmas films—it shows up in everything from *The Bishop's Wife* and *Scrooge* to *A Christmas Story*: It's a shot of children, their noses pressed against the pane of a toyshop window as they gaze longingly at the treasures on display. That shot is neatly parodied in *Jingle All the Way*; here, desperate parents are pressed against the glass door of the toy store, waiting anxiously for the store to open, so that their stampede can begin.

Producer Chris Columbus (director of *Home Alone*, *Mrs. Doubtfire*, and many other hit films) said at the time of production that the film's story line was taken straight from real life. Mentioning that he had spent the previous Christmas searching for a Buzz Lightyear doll (from the Disney film *Toy Story*), Columbus said, "It's almost like searching for a Christmas Eve holy grail—and about as easy. I couldn't find [the Buzz Lightyear doll] anywhere. That was when I came to understand the universality of this situation."

Howard Langston's search is complicated by the presence of Myron Larabee (Sinbad), a tightly wound postal employee who is just as determined to get his hands on a Turbo Man doll as Howard is. "This is the character I've been waiting to play," the six-foot-five comedian said. "I love Myron because he's off-balance and he keeps coming in and out of this relationship with Arnold's character. It's like brotherly hate *and* love—they dig each other, but they don't like each other."

Another Christmas image gets turned on its head when an evil department store Santa (James Belushi) offers Howard a bootleg Turbo Man. To prove that he has one, he has his assistant show Howard a Polaroid shot–ransom style–of the assistant with the doll and the current newspaper. The two then take Howard to a remote toy warehouse operated by dozens of Santas and elves. When the Turbo Man doll, which costs Howard $300, turns out to be Spanish-speaking and in less than mint condition, Howard finds himself in a no-holds-barred brawl with a mob of angry Santas.

Jingle All the Way was filmed in the winter of 1996 at various locations in the Minneapolis-St. Paul area: Linden Hills, Edina, Nicollete Island Park, Rice Park, and at the huge Mall of America, which, at 4.2 million square feet, is the largest enclosed shopping and entertainment complex in the United States.

The elaborate Christmas parade that climaxes *Jingle All the Way* was staged on the "New York Street" at Universal City in Los Angeles. According to the film's press materials, the sequence took three weeks to shoot, as over 1,500 extras sweltered in 100-degree heat while dressed in their wintry best. Marching bands from UCLA and Pasadena City College appeared as the All Santa Marching

Phil Hartman is Ted Maltin, the Langstons' nosy next-door neighbor, in *Jingle All the Way*.

Band and the Turbo Man Band, and a 46-foot long Turbo Man float was created as the parade's centerpiece. The entire parade was then showered with 10,000 pounds of red and gold confetti.

The film's director Brian Levant said, "I really enjoyed staging the Christmas Eve parade. I tried to give it

Rita Wilson portrays Liz Langston, the wife of a well-meaning but neglectful businessman, in *Jingle All the Way*.

a different look and feel, from the choreography to the design of the band costumes and the presentation of the floats; even the color balance of the crowd is something you haven't seen before. I wanted the film to be like a Christmas present–shiny, colorful and wrapped up all nice and neat."

That everything is "wrapped up all nice and neat" is probably the film's biggest failing. The last act of the film is one of those improbability-upon-impossibility plot concoctions that somehow manages to give everyone involved a happy ending. All the zooming and flying and punching and hair-breadth rescues are moderately funny and borderline exciting but not even slightly believable. And if you want to concoct a few moments of warmth and family rec-

Howard Langston (Arnold Schwarzenegger) races across a huge mall on Christmas Eve in a madcap search for the hottest toy of the season in *Jingle All the Way*.

onciliation—as *Jingle All the Way* certainly does—there has to be some reality among the fantasy. This film is far more satisfying to the viewer's emotions than to his intellect.

However, in its relentless and depressing notions of Christmas as a time of panic, greed, and depression, *Jingle All the Way* strikes an uncomfortably familiar chord of truth. *Meet Me in St. Louis* is the Christmas of our dreams; *Jingle All the Way* is, sad to say, Christmas as it really is.

✦   ✦   ✦

PHOTO CREDITS Academy of Motion Picture Arts and Sciences: xiv 20, 131-136 (*except Robinson and Wyatt*), 150 ▪ AIP Video: 86 ▪ American Broadcasting Co.: 149 ▪ Atlantic Entertainment Group: xx (*top*) ▪ Robert S. Birchard: 68, 136 (*Robinson and Wyatt*) ▪ Buena Vista Pictures: 190-191 ▪ Cannon Releasing Corp.: 82-83, 85 ▪ Columbia Pictures: 95-96, 99-100 ▪ Jere Guldin: 8 ▪ Interstar Releasing Corp.: 207-208 ▪ MCA: 91, 101-106, 123, 125 ▪ M-G-M: 44, 60-61 ▪ M-G-M/UA: 45-47, 163-176 ▪ National General: 16-17, 30, 37-38 ▪ Margaret O'Brien: 117 ▪ Paramount Pictures: vi, 24-28, 65-67, 108-110 ▪ Republic Pictures: xii, 147-149 ▪ Samuel Goldwyn: 129, 151 ▪ Frank Thompson: 2-6 ▪ Touchstone Pictures: 154-155 ▪ TriStar Pictures: 58, 63-64, 80, 84 ▪ Turner Entertainment Co.: ii, 10-15, 33, 48-55, 91-94, 97, 112-114, 120, 126-128, 130 ▪ 20th Century-Fox: xvi, xviii, 62, 137-143, 145 (*bottom*), 158-161, 203-206, 213-216 ▪ United Artists: xx (*bottom*), 39-41 ▪ USA Network: 145 (*top*) ▪ Walt Disney Co.: 36, 186-189, 209-211 ▪ Warner Bros.: 70-79, 183-184, 193-197.